The Clarinet

OSKAR KROLL

The Clarinet

Revised, and with a Repertory,
by Diethard Riehm

❀❀❀❀❀

Translated by Hilda Morris

Translation edited by
ANTHONY BAINES

TAPLINGER PUBLISHING COMPANY
New York

First Published in the United States in 1968 by
TAPLINGER PUBLISHING CO., INC.
29 East Tenth Street, New York, New York 10003

Original German edition entitled
Die Klarinette–ihre Geschichte, ihre Literatur,
ihre grossen Meister

© 1965 by Bärenreiter-Verlag, Kassel

Library of Congress Catalog Card Number 68-22701

Printed in Great Britain

PREFACE

In publishing this book I hope to provide clarinettists with all the information they may require about the history of their instrument and its music and literature.

  Much of the contents is based on my own research work and will be of interest to music historians and, above all, to collectors and makers of musical instruments. A good deal has been gleaned from the works of eminent musicologists and great composers, as well as from monographs about the musical history of various cities and dukedoms.

  I trust that this book will be understood and judged not as a scientific work but as a compilation of important facts about the clarinet, its literature and its great virtuosos. Its purpose will have been achieved if it stimulates the clarinettist's interest in the history of his instrument and inspires him to delve more deeply into its valuable solo and chamber music literature.

  I wish to express most cordial thanks to my many friends and helpers for their active support.

Wuppertal, Winter 1944   Oskar Kroll

The intention of Bärenreiter-Verlag to publish this book in the winter of 1944 was frustrated by events during the last months of the war and the severe damage suffered by the firm. My husband did not return from the war. In view of the lapse of time, the manuscript obviously had to be revised, a task undertaken by Diethard Riehm with singular expertise. He has preserved the original conception of the work, as explained by the author in his preface above,

with sympathetic understanding. My best thanks are therefore due
to Mr Riehm.

Wuppertal, Spring 1965   Ilse Kroll

As B. T. Batsford Limited have kindly undertaken to publish an
English edition of this book, I felt it necessary to revise and enlarge
the text. At the request of the publishers I have also added a list of
the most important solo and chamber music works for the clarinet.
It is to be hoped that in the English-speaking world the book will
find many readers and, perhaps, afford some stimulus.

Münster/Westphalia
Am Schlossgarten 34

                                                    Diethard Riehm

CONTENTS

EXPLANATORY NOTES

To indicate positions on the instrument the following terms are used:

Top	—The mouthpiece end
Bottom	—Bell
Front	—The side turned away from the player (the finger-hole side)
Back	—The side nearest the player (the thumb-hole side)
Right hand ⎫ Left ⎭	—As seen by the player
Numbering of holes	—From the bottom upwards

Abbreviations

K	—L. von Köchel's catalogue of Mozart's work
MS	—Manuscript
VfMw	—Vierteljahresschrift für Musikwissenschaft (= quarterly journal of musicology)
Wtq	—A. Wotquenne's thematic catalogue of C. P. E. Bach's works
ZfI	—Zeitschrift für Instrumentenbau (= journal of instrument making)
ZfM	—Zeitschrift für Musik (= journal of music)
ZfMw	—Zeitschrift für Musikwissenschaft (= journal of musicology)

PREDECESSORS AND EARLY FORMS
OF THE CLARINET

Apart from some new and rarely used instruments, the clarinet is one of the youngest members of opera, concert and chamber orchestras. Evolved at the beginning of the eighteenth century, it came into common use only in the second half but then rapidly acquired the position of a leading wind instrument. In terms of the musician's usual classification of musical instruments, it is one of the woodwinds, together with flute, oboe and bassoon. More accurately and in acoustic terms, it belongs in the group of single-reed wind instruments,[1] together with saxophone, tarogato (p. 119) and clarina (p. 119). However, there is a fundamental difference between the clarinet and the other instruments in that group: the other instruments have a markedly conical bore and overblow an octave, while the clarinet in all its larger and smaller forms is preponderately cylindrical and overblows a twelfth. It shares this acoustic property with the stopped organ pipes, and like them produces fundamental notes one octave lower than conical tubes of the same length. This phenomenon explains the extraordinary wide compass of the clarinet compared with other reed instruments and the flute. Acoustically speaking, however, the clarinet does not correspond exactly to the stopped pipe and, although this is often denied, it does possess even-numbered overtones as well as odd.

[1] In contrast to the 'free reed' of the harmonium, this reed is an 'impact tongue', cut from the stems of the plant *Arundo donax L.* (also called Spanish or Italian *Schalmei*, clarinet or giant reed), a native of Mediterranean regions and cultivated particularly in the South of France. Attempts to fashion the reed from other and durable material have not been very successful, though reeds of glass fibre are a fairly efficient substitute for natural reeds (made by Selmer of Paris).

The former tend to be weak in the low register but become increasingly noticeable in the high ones.

Because the clarinet overblows a twelfth, in order to fill out the twelfth chromatically (without forked fingering) it requires at least 18 tone holes, while an instrument which overblows an octave could manage with only 11. That is the reason for the somewhat more difficult fingering of the clarinet compared with the saxophone, the oboe and the flute.

The clarinet represents a coupled system of two vibrating components. The reed, unlike the metal reeds of organ or mouth-organ, is strongly damped in its vibration because it is made of a wood (cane) and the player's lower lip further restrains movement. On the other hand, the vibrations of the air column inside the instrument, which varies in length according to the opening of holes and keys, are only slightly alterable by the reed and therefore determine the coupling frequency, i.e. the resulting tone is governed almost exclusively by the length of the air column and not by the (very high) natural frequency of the reed itself. (The metal reeds of organ, mouth-organ, etc., produce only the pitch to which they are tuned and do not necessarily have to be coupled with an air column.) But a result of this coupling is that the overblown twelfths deviate from the corresponding fundamental notes, i.e. it is impossible, even in theory, to build perfectly-tuned clarinets. Instrument-makers may try to correct this inherent flaw by means of auxiliary keys and special arrangement of holes but ultimately the control lies with the player who has to correct the imperfect utterance by the way he handles his instrument. (As a rule, the notes from *e* to *g* are flat, from *a* to *d'* too sharp, while with the overblown notes demanding the same fingering it is the other way round.)

Instruments of the clarinet family are known to have been used in Egypt from about 2700 B.C. (*memet*) and they were later distributed over the whole of the ancient Mediterranean region. All these instruments, like some still in use today, were double clarinets, i.e. they consisted of two joined tubes, with two mouthpieces. The tubes did not diverge as in the *aulos* (ancient Greek double oboe) but were firmly tied or glued together in a parallel position. These instruments are blown by means of a reed formed by a three-sided cut in the material of the mouthpiece (generally a piece of cane), remaining connected with it at the base. The reed may be cut so that the attached end is uppermost, i.e. nearest the player (in the *zummarah*, fig. 1), or lowermost as in our clarinets (in the *mashurah*). This mouthpiece is inserted into the player's mouth sufficiently far to prevent his tongue or lips touching the reed, which thus vibrates freely. The cavity of the mouth serves merely as a wind chamber. The positions of the holes in the two tubes do not correspond, so that there is a dissonance between the two, and when both are blown together, the resulting tone is harsh.

In another type of double clarinet (*arghul*, fig. 1) the tune is played on one tube while the other produces a drone accompaniment. The drone tube is generally the longer and may reach a length of over three feet. The Sardinian *launedda* has three tubes, two for playing the melody in thirds and sixths, and one for the drone (fig. 1).

Single-tube instruments are preferred in north-east Europe, among them the Russian *brelka* or *zhaleika*, which was later provided with keys and incorporated in the balalaika band; the Hungarian tarogato; and the chalumeau, which probably was a folk instrument as far back as medieval times (although the name could also denote double-tube reed instruments of shawm-like character). The origins of the chalumeau, the predecessor of our clarinet, are uncertain. Perhaps it evolved from a double clarinet through abandonment of the drone tube.

From the point of view of musical history, these folk instruments have not been of any very great importance, but the Central European chalumeau at one time played a part in serious music and later developed into the clarinet through refinements introduced by the Nuremberg instrument-maker J. C. Denner.

That, at least, is the interpretation commonly put on the oldest account of Denner's invention published in J. G. Doppelmayr's work *Nachrichten von den Nürnberger Mathematicis und Künstlern*, 1730, in which the following passage occurs: 'Finally his [Denner's] artistic passion compelled him to seek ways of improving his invention of the aforesaid instrument, and this praiseworthy intention had the desired effect. At the beginning of the current century, he invented a new kind of pipe-work, the so-called clarinet, to the great delight of all music lovers, and at length presented an improved chalumeau.'[1] Unfortunately, we cannot now ascertain the exact nature of Denner's improvements because we know little about the original form of the chalumeau.[2]

It can be said that the chalumeau of Denner's time differed from the clarinet in that it had no barrel and no bell, the treble instrument was much shorter (about 12 inches) and its compass barely exceeded one octave, since it did not overblow. The instrument usually had seven tone-holes. It was then improved (probably by Denner) by the addition of two keys placed front and back above the thumb-hole, which served to increase the compass (f' to a'' or $b''\flat$). Instrument-makers sought to overcome the problem of the narrow compass by providing a family series of instruments. 'It is usual to have treble and alto or *quart*, and even tenor and bass chalumeaux, at either French or German pitch, and by reason of this difficult embouchure they are very hard to play' (J. F. B. C. Majer, *Museum musicum*, Nuremberg, 1732).

Denner probably developed the clarinet from the chalumeau, above all by enabling the instrument to overblow, also widening the bore, lengthening the instrument and providing a bell. The barrel and the mouthpiece were made in one piece. Simple two-key clarinets are known to have originated from Denner's as well as from other contemporary workshops (e.g. Klenig, Oberlender): there is no *proof* that Denner was the first to make clarinets.

The chalumeau was used not infrequently in operas, even long after the invention of the clarinet, e.g. by M. A. Ziani (*Caio Pompilio*, 1704), Antonio Bononcini (*La Conquista delle Spagne*, 1707), A. Ariosti

[1] Zuletzt triebe ihn [namely Denner] sein Kunst-Belieben annoch dahin an, wie er noch ein mehrers durch seine Erfindung und Verbesserung bey bemeldten Instrumenten dargeben mögte, dieses gute Vorhaben erreichte auch würcklich einen erwünschten Effect, indeme er zu Anfang dieses lauffenden Seculi, eine neue Arth von Pfeiffen-Wercken, die so genannte Clarinette, zu der Music-Liebenden großen Vergnügen, ausfande, endlich auch die Chalumeaux verbesserter darstellte.

[2] Many works on the history of musical instruments fix the year of the invention of the clarinet at or about 1690. That date is given in C. G. Murr's *Beschreibung der vornehmsten Merkwürdigkeiten in Nürnberg*, Nuremberg, 1778, which, however, is not as reliable in regard to the history of the clarinet as Doppelmayr's *Nachrichten*, whose author must have known Denner and his sons. Denner died in 1707, so that it must be assumed that the clarinet was invented in the first years of the eighteenth century.

(*Marte placato*, 1707), J. Bonno (*Eleazaro*, 1793), Dittersdorf, Fux (*Giunone placata*, 1725), Hasse (*Alfonso*, 1738, *La Virtù a pie dello croce*, 1737), Keiser (*Serenata*, 1716, draft for *Croesus*), Telemann (in several cantatas and a *Concerto à 9*), Gluck (Vienna *Orfeo*, *Alceste*), Graupner (*Ouverture à 3 chalumeaux*, *Concerto à 2 chalumeaux*, Sonata for chalumeau, viola d'amour and harpsichord, two Trios, Cantatas, and four Concertos for chalumeau), Harrer, Molter, Steffani, Zelenka, König, and others. In 1706, Estienne Roger of Amsterdam advertised *Fanfares et autres airs de chalumeau à 2 dessus* by J. P. Dreux.

In his opera *Il Turno* (originally entitled *Amor vien dal destino*, Düsseldorf, 1709) Agostino Steffani employed four chalumeaux behind the scenes to accompany the song of a faun (the sound of the instruments here was obviously meant to resemble the auloi of the fauns). Steffani uses a quartet of different instruments (first part, $f'–f''$; second, $bb–c''$; third, $c–g''$; the fourth part runs *col basso*, which is executed by two bassoons and two theorbos). The parts are evidently scored for the improved chalumeau with keys, otherwise the compass of the third voice would be inexplicable. Here, as in the operas generally, the chalumeaux are used only in certain numbers for special effects. (For the reference to this opera I am indebted to Professor Dr. Gerhard Kroll of Salzburg—D.R.)

There are no technical difficulties in the chalumeau parts of the above composers. In theoretical literature, the tone colour of the chalumeau is usually not assessed very favourably. Laborde says that it had a 'not very pleasing tone', and in *Das neu-eröffnete Orchester* Mattheson remarks rather maliciously, 'The so-called chalumeaux may be allowed to voice their somewhat howling symphony of an evening, perhaps in June or July and from a distance, but never in January at a serenade on the water.'

On the other hand, it is difficult to believe that an unpleasantly 'howling' instrument with evidently a very strong tone ('from a distance') would have been used by Dittersdorf in a *Divertimento Notturno* (violin, chalumeau, two *Violen*), or by Graupner in a sonata for chalumeau, viola d'amour and harpsichord, i.e. in combination with particularly gentle instruments. Probably the instruments differed a great deal in regard to dimensions, mouthpieces and number of keys, and some may have sounded better than others.[1]

It is not always clear whether the word 'chalumeau' may not have denoted clarinets but double-reed instruments. It should also be noted that in early clarinet parts the direction 'chalumeau' may mean *8va bassa*, i.e. the copyist tried to save ledger-lines and the player had to execute the passage in question one octave lower, in the chalumeau register.

[1] Replicas of the chalumeau may be obtained from the firm of Moeck, Celle, Germany.

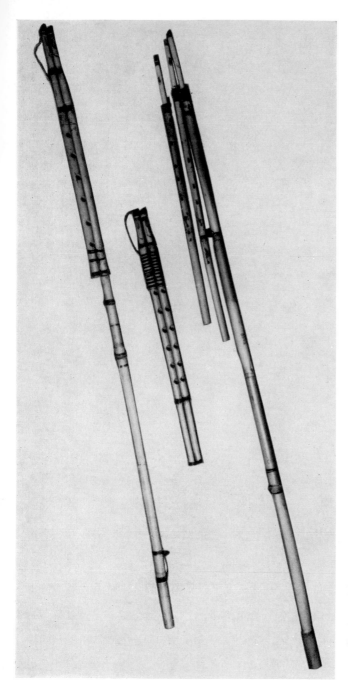

1 Early clarinets (Berlin
Collection).
From left to right: Arghul,
zummarah, launedda.
The mouthpieces show
the downward-pointing
tongues made by a three-
sided cut in the tube

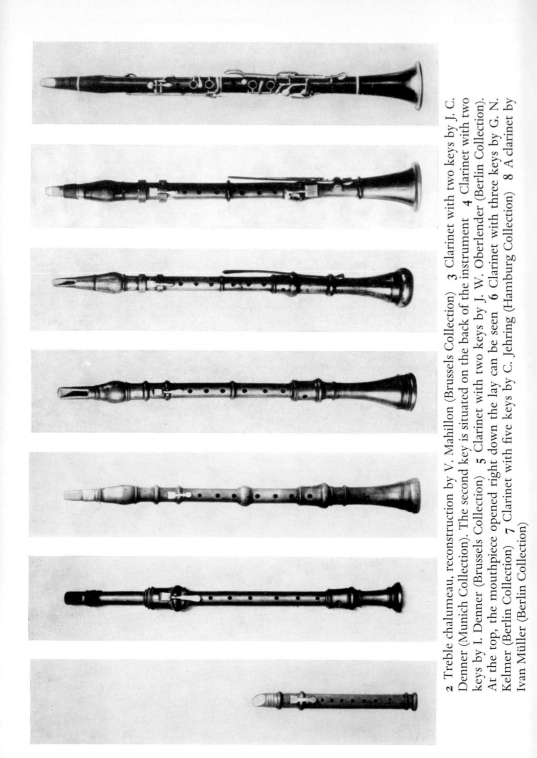

2 Treble chalumeau, reconstruction by V. Mahillon (Brussels Collection) 3 Clarinet with two keys by J. C. Denner (Munich Collection). The second key is situated on the back of the instrument 4 Clarinet with two keys by I. Denner (Brussels Collection) 5 Clarinet with two keys by J. W. Oberlender (Berlin Collection). At the top, the mouthpiece opened right down the lay can be seen 6 Clarinet with three keys by G. N. Kelmer (Berlin Collection) 7 Clarinet with five keys by C. Jehring (Hamburg Collection) 8 A clarinet by Ivan Müller (Berlin Collection)

THE TECHNICAL DEVELOPMENT
OF THE CLARINET

The clarinet in the eighteenth century, its name and early appraisals

The Bavarian National Museum in Munich possesses a perfectly preserved specimen of an early clarinet (no. 136) stamped with the name of J. C. Denner (fig. 3). This instrument is 'undoubtedly the original form of the clarinet and perhaps represents the first attempt to transform the chalumeau' (Mahillon, II, 206). Today this graceful, well-turned instrument is pitched in C, but at the time of manufacture it may well have stood at D in accordance with the lower pitch common in that era. It has eight holes and at its upper end two keys exactly opposite, the one in front being controlled by the index finger and producing $b'\flat$, the one at the back being controlled by the thumb, producing a', and also serving as overblowing key (speaker); if both keys[1] are opened simultaneously, the resulting note is b'. The lowest hole is a so-called twin-hole,[2] i.e. it consists of two small holes in close proximity which, covered separately, produce not the whole-tone but the semitone interval. This clarinet, forked fingering and other auxiliary fingering apart, was capable of the following fundamental tone-series:

[1] Mahillon asserts that their holes had identical diameters and, fingered separately, produced the same note, a. But the Leipzig Museum of Musical Instruments and W. Heckel of Biebrich-am-Rhein (Wiesbaden), both of whom possess replicas of the instrument, have stated that the diameters differed and the notes produced were $b\flat$ and a respectively. Unfortunately, it has not been possible to examine the original instrument.

[2] Instruments still in existence prove, and Schneider also states, that the fifth and sixth holes were sometimes also pierced as twin-holes.

Not all existing two-key clarinets have this scale. To facilitate overblowing, most makers, among them Denner himself and later his sons, put the thumb-key (speaker) higher and narrowed the hole, so that in combination with the front-key, this producing a', it produced only $b'\flat$. This lowering was also promoted by the insertion of a small metal sleeve into the opening of the speaker almost as far as to the central axis of the bore, designed to prevent the entry of water. In addition, it was not long before the diameters of the third and seventh holes were increased, so that the $b\flat/f''$ produced hitherto were now replaced by $b/f''\sharp$, and f'/c''' by $f'\sharp/c'''\sharp$. The exterior of these instruments was improved by widening the lower end of the bore towards the bell.

But a high price had to be paid for thus facilitating the overblow, because now the urgently required note b' was missing. Although by fingering c'' the player could 'by relaxing his lips and drawing back the mouthpiece from his mouth, produce it artificially' (Schneider), the resulting note was very imperfect in regard to pitch and tone. Since the mouthpiece faces were opened further down than is usual today (fig. 5), it was possible to a considerable extent to correct the pitch by the appropriate embouchure. And although clarinets were made whose keys, when fingered simultaneously, produced b', even there the quality left much to be desired. Hence the only possible solution of the problem was to lengthen the instrument and bore a new hole in its lower part, for e/b'.

Histories of musical instruments almost unanimously assert that the lengthening of the clarinet went hand in hand with the higher positioning of the thumb key and that both improvements were due to Jacob Denner, the son of the inventor. However, there is no evidence to support this claim, which rests merely on surmise, because all known Denner clarinets have only the two keys on the upper joint.[1] It is probably now impossible to ascertain who was

[1] The Brussels instrument collection formerly contained (no. 414; Mahillon, I, 430) a three-key Denner clarinet which has regrettably disappeared. It is not certain either

responsible for lengthening the clarinet and thus finally determining the lower limit of its compass. Nor is it known exactly at what time this decisive alteration was first made. Walther and Eisel knew only a two-key clarinet but it is beyond doubt that the three-key instrument (fig. 6) was common around the middle of the eighteenth century, so that it may be assumed that the change took place about 1740.

The position of the holes and the scale remained unaffected by the lengthening of the clarinet, save for the added *e/b′* hole, which on account of its low position[1] had to be covered by a long key manipulated by one thumb.[2] Perhaps two decades passed before the clarinet was furnished with the *g♯/d″♯* and the *f♯/c″♯* keys (fig. 7). From then on the *e/b′* key was actuated by the little finger of the left hand. The *g♯/d″♯* key was first put on the back of the instrument to be accessible to the right thumb but was soon removed to its present place; the *f♯/c″♯* key was always next to the *e/b′* key. It is not known who first provided these two keys. They are said to have been invented by the Brunswick maker Barthold Fritze but this does not seem very likely because, so far as is known, Fritze built only organs and clavichords. Nor is it correct to ascribe the invention to the clarinet virtuoso Joseph Beer, who was born as late as 1744.

The Vienna clarinettist Anton Stadler sought to increase the compass of the instrument in the low register. In co-operation with the maker T. Lotz he lengthened the clarinet by four semitones and introduced the new instrument for the first time on 20 February 1788 at the Vienna Burgtheater, where he performed a concerto on

---

whether it was the work of J. C. or of J. Denner, or whether the third key was original, or—as may well be imagined—a later addition by another maker.

[1] The *f/c″* hole was already on the slant and drilled into a knob in order to be more accessible to the little finger.

[2] At that time the player was free to choose between working the upper joint with the right hand or the left hand, and the lower joint correspondingly with the left or the right hand. The lowest hole was therefore bored in a kind of 'bulb', which the player could turn to either side as he liked. With the invention of the *e/b′* key this arrangement ceased and an *f/c″* hole was then bored on each side of the instrument. The player was left to close one of them with wax or a spindle-shaped wooden plug. The only exception is to be seen in instrument no. 150 in the Germanisches Museum at Nuremberg, where, according to the positioning of the hands and the setting of the 'barrel', the long key may be worked by either the left thumb or the left little finger.

Applicatio auf das Clarinett.

§. 16.

Clarinetto, ist ein zu Anfang dieses Seculi von einem Nürnberger erfundenes/ und einer langen Hautbois nicht ungleiches hölzernes Blass Instrument, ausser daß ein breites Mundstück daran befestiget ist; es klingt dieses Instrument von ferne einer Trompete ziemlich ähnlich/ und gehet von dem Tenor f. biß zum 2. gestrichenen a. auch zuweilen ins 3. gestrichene c.

Das

Fingering chart of a two-key clarinet, from Majer's *Museum musicum*, 1732 (for translation see facing page)

The clarinet is a woodwind instrument invented at the beginning of this century by a Nuremberger. It resembles a long oboe, except for a wide mouthpiece; from afar the instrument sounds not unlike a trumpet. Its compass extends from tenor f to a'', occasionally to c'''.

Left hand
- Thumb-key
- Thumb-hole
- Index finger — Key / Hole
- Middle finger
- Ring finger

Right hand
- Index finger
- Middle finger
- Ring finger
- Little finger

Musical scale with note names

F G G♯ A B♭ B C C♯ D D♯ E F F♯ G   A B♭ B C C♯ D D♯ E F F♯ G G♯ A

this so-called 'bass clarinet'.[1] But the instrument failed to find favour and has apparently not been preserved in any collection. Mozart used Stadler's invention in the original version of his Clarinet Concerto, in some short fragments, and in *La Clemenza di Tito* and *Così fan tutte*. In addition, the Quintet was almost certainly written for the Stadler-Lotz clarinet. We shall return to this question later (p. 61).

About 1791 the Parisian clarinet virtuoso Jean Xavier Lefèvre added a sixth key to the existing five, for $c'\sharp/g''\sharp$, and the clarinet remained essentially at this stage of development until the great reforms of Ivan Müller. Almost simultaneously with Lefèvre some other makers provided this sixth key, e.g. Dupré of Tournay, N. M. Raingo of Mons, and Kerkhove of Ghent (Altenburg, *ZfI*. 25, 891).

A six-key clarinet did exist before Lefèvre but we do not know the functions of the various keys, especially of the sixth. An article 'L'art du faiseur d'instruments de musique' in the *Encyclopédie* of Diderot and d'Alembert, published 1751–1780, contains the following passage: 'As I was writing this article, a musician passed through Berlin with a six-key clarinet on which he was able to perform in every key. Everyone knows the difficulties caused by four keys; with six it must be even worse.' Today that seems a strange statement to make, but it should be remembered that the felt pads used in those days did not close the holes as tightly as modern leather or skin pads and, therefore, that it was desirable, as far as possible, to exclude unreliable mechanism and noisy keys. But the remark also underlines the problem inherent in the clarinet: the impossibility of playing equally fluently and truly in every key. To this day makers have sought to solve the problem by various means, by constantly adding new keys and lever-connections and by other experiments. One way of overcoming the difficulty was early seen,

---

[1] The *Journal des Luxus und der Moden*, 1801, p. 543, reported: 'Herr Stadler, a great virtuoso of several wind instruments, presented himself at one of the academies [concerts] performed by amateurs in the Augarten. He played a clarinet with modifications of his own invention. His instrument is not of the usual uniform shape throughout. About three-quarters of its length down it has a ridge running round the tube which from that point onward flares out towards the bell [durch den letztern vierten Theil ungefähr ist eine Querrippe angebracht, von welcher aus erst die weiter hinausgebogene hervorragende Öffnung geht]. This has the advantage of giving the instrument more range in the lower register, and the lowest notes sound not unlike those of a French horn.'

namely in making clarinets of different pitches, but this only led to fresh problems. For one thing, the average musician cannot afford to buy a whole set of instruments;[1] for another, playing becomes very awkward when the musician has to change constantly from one instrument to another, the mouthpieces in some cases being of different sizes and the reeds responding differently. In addition, he experiences tuning problems when he has to exchange an instrument warmed up by playing for another one which is still cold. So makers adopted a primitive expedient: they provided the clarinet with certain joints of varying lengths, so that the player, by exchanging these joints, could retune his instrument from A to B♭ or from B♭ to C. Certainly these instruments would have shown very uncertain tuning but the light reeds of those days would have made it possible to regulate the intonation by lip pressure.

As late as 1855, H. W. von Gontershausen wrote in *Magazin musikalischer Tonwerkzeuge*: 'The main reason for using a set of clarinets lies in the fact that one and the same instrument cannot easily be played in every tonality. There is still this fault in the instrument but it brings the advantage that the various members of the set produce different timbres. Next to the flute, the clarinet is the most popular of wind instruments. In solemn hymn as in festive procession, in the concert as in the opera, and even in the military band, it plays the most brilliant part in that it usually represents the principal voice. It is the breadwinner of the itinerant musician and sweetens the lowly life of the solitary shepherd. Thus, the manufacture of and trade in clarinets are of some importance and produce considerable profit.'

Early opinions of the clarinet were not particularly favourable. 'From a distance it sounds rather like a trumpet', wrote Walther, and many authors of musical-history books have since quoted him verbatim.[2] The clarinet did not come into its own until in the age of sensibility there gradually awakened a liking for its warm, sensual tones, though as late as 1795 J. E. Altenburg wrote in his book *Versuch einer Anleitung zur heroisch-musikalischen Trompeter- und*

---

[1] Although then, as now, large orchestras provided their players with these very expensive instruments.

[2] Compare, for instance, Eisel and Majer.

Pauker-Kunst: 'The strident and piercing sound of this instrument is most useful in the military music of the infantry; and it sounds much better from afar than close to.'

The mordant, bright, sound which the clarinet undoubtedly had in early times, was responsible for its name. The word 'clarinet' is a diminutive of the Italian *clarino*, used for the high solo trumpets.[1] We do not know who first named the clarinet, but as the oldest account of Denner's invention already mentions the name, it is not impossible that Denner himself or his sons were responsible for it.[2]

Ivan Müller's reform

Lefèvre's sixth key had eased the task of the clarinettist in many ways but virtuosi and composers were still far from satisfied with the technical possibilities and the purity and quality of tone. Some makers tried to correct specific faults but no one was prepared to undertake the necessary overall reform. Carl Gollmick wrote in 1845: 'Although some instrument-makers were anxious to improve an imperfect or thoroughly wrong note by new holes and keys, and sometimes achieved the desired result, the position of the keys made them difficult to control, so that any advantage was largely wiped out. Besides, even if this problem were completely solved, i.e. if a hole and key were provided for every imperfect note, all would still not be well. The underlying and cardinal fault of the instrument lay in the way it was made. The relations of length to width, and of both to the lay-out of the middle section and the finger-holes was wrong. Some of the holes were too small, others too big, which naturally led to a total unevenness of the notes produced. Purity

[1] The similarity and affinity of the words 'clarinets' and 'clarini' has given rise to many errors and misunderstandings. Throughout the eighteenth century the words were often used in a misleading manner; there are, for instance, 'clarini' parts meant for clarinets, and 'clarinet' parts which could be executed only by high solo trumpets, namely *clarini*. (For example, in his opera *La speranza assicurata*, composed in 1736, J. G. Reuter does not use clarinets, but clarino trumpets (VfMw. 8, 297).) Only from 1770 onwards has the word 'clarinet' been confined to its present meaning (Cucuel).

[2] When Reichardt was director of the Berlin Opera Orchestra (1776–94), the clarinet had its place immediately next to the brass because, as suggested by its name, the instrument was regarded as a relative of the clarino trumpet.

and evenness of tone, the aim of every singer, instrumentalist and virtuoso, have up to now been missing in the clarinet. For a long time no one was found who, in the interest of art, would undertake a thorough reform.'

The demand for purity and evenness of all notes was not universal at that time; thus, prominent flautists of the nineteenth century resisted the introduction of the Boehm flute because they regarded the uniform timbre and volume of the notes produced by it as a fault and claimed that it sounded 'monotonous' (Fürstenau). Even Hans von Bülow spoke disparagingly of the Boehm flute with its 'clarinet tone'.

As early as 1791 the Berlin maker Floth built a clarinet with eight keys and in 1809 Baermann had a 10-key clarinet built in Berlin. Outside Germany also, eminent makers strove to improve the clarinet. In 1800 James Wood in England took out a patent for a seventh, $g'\sharp$, key to be manipulated by the right hand; in 1808 J. F. Simiot of Lyons invented the trill key for $a'-b'$ and $b'\flat-c'$. At the same time he lined the g' hole with a small tube to prevent the outflow of water, and, for the same reason, transferred the hole for the speaker key to the front of the instrument. Twenty years later, Simiot even built a clarinet with 19 keys.

In 1808 a clarinet enthusiast published an article in the *Allgemeine Musikzeitung*, demanding at least nine keys for a good clarinet. Spohr, in the introduction to his Clarinet Concerto, composed in the same year, emphasised that it could be executed only with an instrument possessing the following keys: an $e'\flat/b''\flat$ key for the second finger of the right hand, an f'/c''' key for the third finger of the left hand, and trill key for $a'-b'$ and $b'\flat-c''$, a $g\sharp$ key and a key for $b\flat/f''$, in addition to a twin hole or a key to produce $c'\sharp/g''\sharp$, and a hole for the right thumb to produce b.[1]

Ivan Müller must have been familiar with the efforts of makers when he set out to improve the clarinet in 1806.[2] Three years later he was appointed to a post in Paris, where, at that time, the most

---

[1] A clarinet made for the Duke of Sondershausen (in the hunting lodge of Possen), probably to specifications by Hermstedt, does not have this last hole.

[2] He had previously done some work to improve the bassoon and provided three new keys (Müller, *Anweisung*).

outstanding woodwind-makers had their workshops, and tried to make his invention known there. However, it can hardly be assumed that at that point his work was completed because another six years passed before he submitted his 'new clarinet' and the *Clarinette alto* to a committee of experts in 1812. The committee's conclusions were full of misapprehensions and so unfavourable that Müller's newly-founded instrument works had to close down. Nevertheless, a few years later J. B. Gambaro and Frédéric Berr[1] used the new instruments with sensational effect, and Müller's improvements were copied elsewhere with varying success.

It was Ivan Müllers' intention to make a 'new' clarinet with uniform quality of tone and true tuning. At the same time, he wished to increase its technical capabilities, so that the player might dispense with a whole set of clarinets and play compositions in any tonality on the B♭ clarinet, which was 'about midway in pitch among the others'. This was one of the reasons why the committee which, after all, had members like Cherubini and Méhul, rejected Müller's clarinet. It was reluctant to forgo the various tone colours of the C, B♭ and A clarinets. However, he was careful, 'not to do anything which might interfere with the former use or technique; all previously familiar fingerings have not only been preserved but, so far as seemed possible, applied' (Müller, *Anweisung*). Müller's reform was a brilliant success and for many years to come, despite later improvements, his clarinet amply satisfied the needs of smaller orchestras. The inventor himself kept an open mind for additional innovations and worked to the end of his life to improve his instrument. He experimented with new keys and also made use of the ring-key system.[2]

The following illustrates the function and fingering of the 13 keys of Müller's clarinet (thumb reckoned as first finger):

1.	*e/b'*	5th finger, left hand
2.	*f♯/c"♯*	5th finger, left hand, and right thumb
3.	*f/c"*	5th finger, right hand
4.	*g♯/d"♯*	5th finger, right hand and right thumb

---

[1] Prominent clarinettists of the Théâtre Italien in Paris.

[2] As shown by his instrument made by Schuster of Markneukirchen which is to be found in the Berlin collection (no. 789), see fig. 8.

5.	*bb/f″*	4th finger, right hand
6.	*b/f″♯*	5th finger, right hand
7.	*c′♯/g″♯*	5th finger, left hand
8.	*e′b/b″b*	4th finger, left hand
9.	*f′/c‴*	2nd finger, right hand
10.	*g′♯*	2nd finger, left hand
11.	*a′*	2nd finger, left hand
12.	*a′/b′* trill	2nd finger, right hand
13.	Speaker key	left thumb

The second and fourth keys each required a thumb branch (as indicated above) because rollers had not yet been invented.[1] The sixth key served to correct *b/f″♯*; it was later replaced by the *Brille* (lit., spectacles) with an open key. The eleventh key simultaneously opened the tenth; Müller considered it impractical to separate the two, as also to provide for actuation of the eighth key (or a lever connected with it) by the right index finger, because it would have been 'a hindrance in various situations, if not altogether unusable'. In order to obviate the lining tube of the speaker key, Müller transferred its hole to the left side of the instrument. Hitherto it had normally been situated at the back.

Müller introduced an important innovation in regard to the pads. His pads were made of gut or leather stuffed with wool, as generally used today. Earlier pads consisted of slices of soft leather or felt, stuck with glue or sealing wax to the underside of the flap. Müller wrote in this connection: 'In regard to the keys, I have invented a kind of elastic "ball" and, having used it for several years, I am convinced of its efficacy. There is no risk with these pads that either a moist or a dry atmosphere will make the keys unworkable; they close the holes effectively under all conditions and make no noise.'

Müller was also one of the first clarinettists to decry the curious habit of controlling the reed by the pressure of the upper lip, which was common practice at that time, and in his *Anweisung* he

---

[1] The rollers were invented in 1823 by C. Janssen, a clarinettist at the Paris Opéra Comique, and at first were used, not very successfully, for the two keys worked by the little finger of the left hand. Later they were introduced more generally and replaced Müller's branches.

described the disadvantages of this method. Baermann and Berr later followed his arguments in their great Tutors, as J. Fröhlich had, somewhat earlier, in his *Systematischer Unterricht*. However, in Spain and Italy the old practice continued for a long time, not only among clarinettists in small bands but even among first-rate players in good orchestras. Thus, H. Gräff reported (*ZfI*. 1, 168) that he heard —probably about 1880—the solo clarinettist of a municipal opera perform the 'Variations' by Cavallini 'with terrific technique' by this method, although it sounded as though the soloist were playing on the 'glottis of a goose' rather than on the mouthpiece of a clarinet. A prospectus of the firm of Maino and Orsi in Milan depicted a 'clarinetto a doppia tonalità', invented in 1887, with reed turned towards the front. But today Italian players have adopted the habit of blowing with the reed 'downwards', as Backofen called it, namely against the lower lip.

In his clarinet Tutor of 1824, Backofen reported that about 50 per cent of all clarinettists still played with the reed upwards, a technique which does not allow of the brilliant tongued staccato, although it favours play in the high register and a production resembling that of the human voice ('lung staccato'). In more recent times, Ferdinando Busoni, Ferrucio's father, in his clarinet Tutor of 1883, again pleaded in favour of 'playing reed upwards'.

In 'playing downwards' it was not the usual technique, as it is today, to place the upper teeth directly on the mouthpiece but to interpose the upper lip. On the other hand, Carl Baermann's Tutor emphatically condemns this method.

The decades of Müller's reforms also produced various other inventions and improvements, the exact dates of which are now uncertain, e.g. the thumb rest, originally carved out of the tube itself but later made of ivory or metal. The screw ligature, which underwent several alterations over the years, was introduced about the same period. It has never really taken hold in Germany but is used almost exclusively elsewhere, particularly in the Latin countries and in Britain.

Several players and makers of this period also sought to improve the mouthpiece, the construction of which was extremely primitive in the early instruments. Looking at them now, it is easy to see why the early clarinets did not have the mellow tone of modern instruments. In the first place, the early mouthpieces were open down the whole length of the lay, so that the reed rested on a narrow table and had a somewhat precarious hold. Secondly, the mouthpieces were much too small, reaching barely the size of a modern bassoon reed! These faults were soon corrected by the experts. Next, a way had to be found to prevent the warping of the lay, for which purpose a piece of metal was affixed to the mouthpiece;[1] but it soon transpired that mouthpieces treated in this way tended to split when exposed to excessive humidity or a dry atmosphere for any length of time. Makers then began to experiment with different materials thought to be impervious to moisture, such as glass,[2] china, marble,[3] ivory and metal.[4] But all proved to be unsuitable in some respect and the experiments produced no useful results. The ebonite mouthpiece, still the most popular with many players, was not introduced until the seventies of the last century. Since 1937 several German makers and musicians have been experimenting with mouthpieces and even whole instruments made of plexiglass.[5] Wooden mouthpieces, generally of cocus or grenadilla, and those of other synthetic materials are still popular.

 The greatest problem remained the profile of the lay of the mouthpiece, whose more or less gently descending course must bear a specific relation to the strength of the reed. But the structure of the cane differs from piece to piece and it is therefore impossible to make reeds conforming in every detail to a pattern. F. Triébert hit on the idea of a lay which could be adjusted by the player to suit the reed. The invention was patented in 1847 and

---

[1] Manufactured, amongst others, by Stengel of Bayreuth, H. J. Ziegler of Vienna, and H. F. Czermak of Prague.

[2] First produced by Szalkiewicz of Warsaw.

[3] C. Baermann is thought to have experimented with this material, and Giovanni Ugolini of Florence manufactured mouthpieces of *pietra dura* (marble).

[4] Hermstedt had mouthpieces made of silver, also of bell metal (the latter produced a 'bell-like metallic tone'), with a gold-lined lay. Sax, too, made metal mouthpieces. Today they are occasionally used for saxophones.

[5] At the Paris World Exhibition of 1937, plexiglass instruments caused a sensation and earned much praise. The author has on several occasions performed at chamber music concerts on a plexiglass A clarinet made by Clemens Wurlitzer of Wernitzgrün, and has been very satisfied with it.

later taken up by other instrument makers[1] but the result was never satisfactory.

In 1891 the Paris firm of Thibouville turned out a very curious item called the *mégalophone*. This was a mouthpiece containing spiral grooves not unlike those in a gun barrel. They were supposed to produce greater volume and fluency of emission but the invention never gained recognition. More important was the thorough reform undertaken later by Oskar Oehler who invented the 'curved lay' (*geschweifte Bahn*), on which the reed, to heighten its elasticity and capacity to vibrate, is firmly tied to the lay by means of a cord (preferable to a ligature for such a lay). Today this method is widely used by German and many other clarinettists.

Early clarinets were mainly of light-coloured boxwood (*Buxus*), sometimes pear or maple wood, or even of ivory. The brown cocus wood (*Brya ebenus*) was in vogue for a long time but is today used mainly for mouthpieces and bells (because of its light weight). The most common material now is grenadilla (usually *Dalbergia melanoxylon*) which is naturally of a dark colour (often dyed black, though there is an occasional brown clarinet with gilded mechanism). Grenadilla is very heavy but impervious to moisture and changes in temperature. Clarinets of metal or ebonite for outdoor bands are quite unaffected by climatic conditions. The material of a clarinet has much less influence on the tone than is usually imagined, because, despite a belief held by many clarinettists, the tube itself hardly vibrates at all, only the air column inside. The condition of the inner wall (i.e. degree of smoothness), however, plays a considerable part.

The influence of the Boehm flute

After the first quarter of the nineteenth century, Ivan Müller's system gained general recognition and was adopted by the majority of clarinettists. Then Theobald Boehm published his invention of the Boehm flute, which was to conquer the musical world. Two far-sighted clarinettists and makers immediately recognised that

[1] Mahillon of Brussels, Kruspe of Erfurt, and Josef Grämer of Graslitz.

this system had a direct bearing on the clarinet and held out un-expected promise for its future development. Naturally, Boehm's ideas could not entirely be applied to the clarinet, which is based on totally different acoustic principles from the flute; fundamentally, the so-called Boehm clarinet[1] adopted from the Boehm flute only the ring-keys and some details of the fingering.

Ring-keys were made as early as 1808 by the Rev. Frederick Nolan, and in 1824 Pottgiesser carried out similar experiments with crescent-shaped plates, to be followed by the work of Gordon, which Boehm later took over. Probably proceeding from these early trials, Lefèvre made a clarinet with a ring-key in 1826 or even earlier, for the clarinettist Blève of Le Havre, but this experiment came to nothing. However, the close collaboration of the clarinet-tist H. E. Klosé with the maker L. A. Buffet Jnr., both of Paris, produced the *clarinette à anneaux mobiles*[2] which we know today as the Boehm clarinet.

In the introduction to his great clarinet Tutor (1844), Klosé gives the following account of his novel ideas and collaboration with Buffet: 'When I followed Berr as teacher at the Royal Conserva-toire, it was my greatest wish conscientiously to carry out the many duties of my teaching post. I also desired to bring the clarinet to the prominence it so richly deserves on account of the beauty of its tone and its capacity as a leading as well as an accompanying instru-ment. Therefore, I had first to try to remove the various weak-nesses from which the instrument still suffered. For a long time I worked on the realisation of this idea and conducted many experi-ments. I considered that the ring-key mechanism offered the best solution to all the difficulties I had been working for years to over-come. M. Auguste Buffet showed a happy understanding of my ideas and was able to put them into practice. To him I owe the instrument which I now venture to present to professional and amateur musicians.'

In 1839[3] Buffet first exhibited, together with some Boehm flutes

---

[1] The name 'Boehm clarinet' was probably introduced in the 1860s by Mollenhauer.
[2] 'Clarinet with movable rings'.
[3] Shortly afterwards Buffet, after many experiments, introduced the needle-springs which are in common use today.

from his workshop, a clarinet 'made in accordance with the same system which, however, M. Boehm has not hitherto tried to apply to the clarinet'. Five years later, when he had applied Boehm's mechanism to the oboe, he was granted a patent for these instruments (1844). It seems that no Boehm clarinet of this period has been preserved. But the drawings in the letters patent and Klosé's Tutor show that the first Boehm clarinets had the same number of keys in the same positions as today. That certain details may have been altered and improved since does not detract from the greatness of an invention which has proved its excellence over a period of more than 100 years and has found its way all over the world.

The Buffet-Klosé instruments represented an important advance not only in musical and technical terms. The exterior appearance of the clarinet was also much improved: it assumed a more graceful look as the ungainly block and collar bearings disappeared and the keys themselves were fashioned much more delicately. The two inventors made use of end-pivoted keys, which further improved the appearance of the instrument.

Simultaneously with Buffet and Klosé, an improved clarinet was introduced by Adolphe Sax, whose part in the development of the instrument is an outstanding one. At the early age of 21 (1835) he had constructed a clarinet with 24 keys[1] which, however, failed to succeed, in spite of an 'honourable mention' at the Belgian industrial exhibition. In 1839 he introduced a completely changed instrument. No details of its construction are known but it may safely be assumed that it was the predecessor of the clarinet models patented in 1840 and 1842. In contrast to Buffet and Klosé, Sax retained Ivan Müller's fingering but he introduced some improvements of the greatest significance. Above all, he removed one obstacle to fluent playing by replacing the $b/f''\sharp$ key by automatic open '*Brille*'—an important innovation which was soon in common use with makers of all countries the world over. The second improvement was less successful: Sax extended the compass

---

[1] In 1828 Simiot demonstrated to the Academy of Fine Arts in Paris a 19-key clarinet which received much praise for its well-thought-out and progressive construction.

9 Clarinet on the Romero system by E. Albert, Brussels **10** Clarinet by Oskar Oehler, Berlin (1902) **11a, b** A and B♭ clarinets by Oskar Oehler, Berlin (1930) **12** Schmidt Reform Boehm clarinet by Fritz Wurlitzer, Erlbach (1942) **13** Quarter-tone clarinet by Fritz Schüller, Markneukirchen

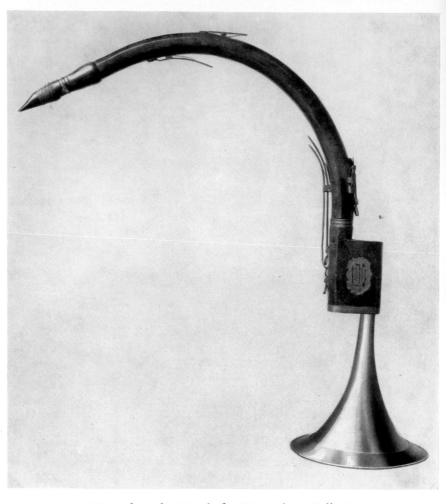

14 Basset horn by Mayrhofer (Nuremberg Collection)

to low $e\flat$, which is only seldom found today.[1] Among various minor alterations, Sax also introduced the second speaker key, later adopted and variously modified by several makers and most useful in bass clarinets. However, in spite of undoubted merits, the Sax clarinet never gained a firm foothold.

Yet other instrument makers and clarinettists also worked on the application of the ring-key to the clarinet. Thus, in 1845 Buffet-Crampon,[2] together with Blancou, constructed the *clarinette omni-tonique*,[3] which combined Müller's system with the facilities effected by Boehm's invention. In 1853 the clarinettist Antonio Romero y Andia invented an ingenious instrument designed to play in any tonality without technical difficulties. Paul Bié, then owner of Lefèvre's firm, constructed these clarinets in 1862–64, and four years later, and again about 1890, simplified their extremely complicated mechanism. But the Romero clarinet never became a success. The system improved many notes and removed a number of difficulties but it demanded a complete change of fingering. Its most significant innovation consisted in the manipulation of the keys for $g'\sharp$, a' and $b'\flat$, through a lever and spring system, by the three ring-keys of the lower joint (fig. 9). Almost at the same time, V. Mahillon of Brussels made an instrument resembling the Romero clarinet, although he knew nothing of the Spaniard's work.

The so-called $b'/c''\sharp$ trill should be mentioned as a very important French invention, representing a considerable simplification compared with Boehm's system. The mechanism, which may be seen today on almost all clarinets of 'German' construction,[4] consists of a second, open-standing, $c''\sharp$ key coupled with the b' and c'' keys

---

[1] The low $e\flat$ makes it possible for A clarinet passages to be played on B$\flat$ clarinets, which is not infrequently done in Britain and U.S.A. Some composers demand the note, e.g. Mahler in the *Song of the Earth* and Busoni, though *ad lib.*, in the *Concertino*; normally, it should not be required by composers any more than the low c on the bass clarinet.

Some German makers and amateurs have tried to increase the compass of the Oehler clarinet to $e\flat$ by inserting a so-called 'lower barrel' between the bell and lower joint. German clarinets with low $e\flat$ are made, amongst others, by Georg Grässel.

[2] A nephew of L. A. Buffet.

[3] 'Clarinet for all tonalities'.

[4] Many German clarinettists have this mechanism arranged in such a way that it can be put in or out of operation as desired.

and actuated from the *b'* position by raising the little finger of the right hand, the *c"* key, through a lever connecting it with *b'*, meanwhile remaining closed.

Countless other inventions and improvements were introduced during this period by French and Belgian makers but space prohibits an appreciation or even the mention of every inventor, especially as the instruments in question failed to stand the test of time and are not preserved in any collection of musical instruments. Pierre, Pontécoulant and Mahillon give detailed accounts of many of these experiments.

In Britain, too, many clarinet systems were developed only to prove unsuccessful in the long run. Here, too, the Boehm clarinet is by far the most popular. In 1858 Richard Carte conducted a most interesting experiment with a clarinet, adhering strictly to Boehm's principles. While the mechanism of the lower joint was an almost exact replica of that on instruments by Buffet-Klosé, the fingering of the upper joint differed considerably from any other known system, which was the reason why the instrument failed to meet with success. For example, the *a'*, *g'♯* and speaker keys were open-standing and had to be closed by means of ring-keys controlled by various fingers of both hands. The instrument never influenced any further developments.

More lasting success was achieved by an invention of the oboe virtuoso Apollon Barret, which made possible or facilitated some trills on the upper joint of the clarinet. Depression of a certain lever by the right index finger releases ring-keys, whereupon the fingering *d'*/*a"* produces *e'♭*/*b"♭*, and the fingering *e'*/*b"* produces *f'*/*c'''*. As the depression of the lever does not affect the fingering of *c'*/*g"*, it is possible, or very much easier, to execute the trills and tremolos *c'*/*e'♭*, *c'*/*f'*, *e'♭*/*f'*, etc. A further change affects the fingering of the *g'♯* key which is worked not by the index finger of the left hand but by the second finger; in addition, the *e*/*b'* and the *f♯*/*c'♯* keys are arranged one below the other, instead of side by side, and there are rollers to the *c'♯*/*g"♯* key. The Barret system came into use not only in Britain but also in Holland. Later, G. A. Clinton introduced some improvements to both the Barret and the Boehm systems, and his instruments were once popular in Britain.[1]

The clarinets used in Britain, France and the U.S.A. are almost exclusively of the Boehm type, while the German system is preferred in Germany, Austria and neighbouring countries. The objection of German orchestral clarinettists to the Boehm system is based not so much on the fingering, which is in some respects superior to the German system, obviating, for instance, the sliding of the little fingers from one key to another, but on the timbre, which is not affected by the arrangement of the keys. As a rule, the Boehm clarinets available on the market have to be played with special mouthpieces, which, in turn, require lighter reeds. Thus, the German player has to adjust both his fingering technique and his embouchure. The Boehm clarinet has a wide mouthpiece with an open lay and a light, wide reed, while the Oehler clarinet requires a mouthpiece with close lay and a heavy, narrow reed. In addition, the bore of the Boehm clarinets is often rather different and the holes are smaller. In conjunction with the special mouthpieces and lays, this produces a brighter, thinner, though also smoother and more uniform tone colour. On the whole, German clarinettists prefer the slightly less homogeneous but darker, rounder tone of German clarinets. (Analogous differences in tone colour are also often found between oboes and bassoons of German and French build.)

Although present-day clarinettists in the Latin and Anglo-Saxon countries use the Boehm clarinet and its variants to the exclusion of almost any other, it should not be assumed that its adoption was easy or rapid. Indeed, initial resistance to the instrument was considerable and several decades passed before the new system finally established itself. It is altogether surprising to note how long primitive instruments remained in use side by side with the more sophisticated forms. For example, as late as the 1840s the Italian virtuoso E. Cavallini insisted on playing a six-key clarinet; a finger-

---

[1] In 1892 P. Pupeschi invented an improvement for the slur from $c''\sharp$ to $g''\sharp$. The $c'\sharp/g''\sharp$ lever for the little finger of the left hand was omitted altogether. These notes were made by depressing either of the other keys controlled by the little finger of the left hand (i.e. e/b' or $f\sharp/c''\sharp$). Thus, slurs like $b'-g''\sharp$ or $c''\sharp-g''\sharp$ became easily possible. Many saxophones have a similar mechanism, though with adjunction of a $g''\sharp$ lever.

ing chart by Grosse, published by Merseburger in 1894, is based on
the single-brille instrument; and almost incredibly primitive types
were offered and sought in the columns of musical journals of that
period.

German clarinettists have continued to resist the Boehm clarinet
to this day[1] but improvements carried out by French makers
nevertheless left their mark on German instruments, many German makers having received their training in Paris, for many years
the home of the most renowned woodwind makers. For example,
German makers and clarinettists early recognised the advantages
of the ring-key system, and Ivan Müller himself was one of the first
to use it. Indeed, that innovation very rapidly found general recognition and today a clarinet without ring-keys, i.e. without brille,
would be unthinkable and useless. However, in other respects,
German makers developed their own system, based mainly on the
instrument invented by Ivan Müller.

It was chiefly Carl Baermann who, in collaboration with the
maker Ottensteiner, improved the Müller clarinet. Thanks to its
considerable advantages over the older system, this instrument,
under the designation of 'Baermann clarinet', was rapidly adopted
all over Germany, especially since Baermann's excellent clarinet
Tutor was based on it. Baermann's fingering made playing much
easier because, by means of auxiliary levers, most keys could be
controlled from different positions or were provided twice over.
Thus, a lever soldered to the $c'\sharp/g''\sharp$ key[2] made it workable by the
right index finger; $e'\flat/b''\flat$ could be made by the fourth or third
finger of the left hand, as well as by the right index finger; and a
lever was added by which the fourth finger of the left hand could
open the f'/c''' key. A new $b\flat/f''$ lever was provided for the little
finger of the left hand, also a second trill key for the right index
finger. Ring-key mechanisms corrected the notes $f'\sharp$ and $b/f''\sharp$. It

---

[1] The Leipzig clarinettist Traugott Gentzsch adopted the Boehm system as early as
the 1880s, and his son-in-law and successor at the conservatoire, Professor Edmund
Heyneck, also favoured its adoption. A pupil of his, Ernst Schmidt, was particularly
enthusiastic in his support for the Boehm system. His work will be discussed in detail
later.

[2] Bischoff of Darmstadt had earlier provided such a lever but later it was replaced
by an auxiliary lever for the left thumb.

was on such an instrument that Richard Mühlfeld played Brahms's compositions.

Towards the end of the last century, Robert Stark and the maker Anton Osterried further refined the Baermann clarinet, basing some of their improvements on the Boehm system. First they corrected the position of the second trill key, enabling it to produce a trill in true pitch and, in combination with the a' key, a more sonorous $b'♭$. A further improvement facilitated the execution of the trills $b'/c''♯$ and $c''♯/d''$: the right thumb could actuate two levers, connected with the b' and the c'' keys respectively; and by the use of these levers, it was possible to trill either to $c''♯$ with the little finger of the left hand, or to $d''♯$ with the little finger of the right hand. This device was later replaced by the French mechanism already described. Stark also tried to provide the Baermann clarinet with an $f''♯/g''♯$ trill by fitting a second $g''♯$ key, connected by lever with $f''♯$. While this extra key was opened by the left thumb, placing the right index finger on the first brille ring, i.e. the fingering for $f''♯$, closed it again. Stark abolished the $b♭/f''$ and $a♭/e''♭$ levers for the little finger of the left hand.

Combination clarinets

Almost every musician and maker striving to improve the clarinet aimed at an instrument which would enable the player to satisfy any demand of composers in regard to fingering and to play in every tonality, and thus to obviate the necessity of using several instruments and the resulting difficulties. It was recognised early on that the problem could not be solved by increasing the number of keys and complicating the lever connections to facilitate auxiliary fingering. Therefore, some ingenious musicians and makers tried to overcome the difficulties by the construction of 'combination' or 'double-pitch' clarinets.

Probably the first attempt in this direction was undertaken by J. F. Simiot who, in 1808, constructed a C clarinet which, by means of 10 extension joints distributed over the whole length of the instrument, could be turned into a B♭ clarinet. In the 1830s similar experiments were carried out by the Berlin chamber musician Sundelin and, in 1841, by the maker Stövecken of Rheine. In collaboration with the Munich maker Pentenrieder, Carl Baermann also constructed a combination clarinet which, however, as he himself admitted, proved quite useless because of its excessive weight due to the many keys. J. S. Hermstedt was another musician who worked on the problem. He built a clarinet in which mouthpiece and barrel were connected by a screw-thread. In addition, there was a slide joint in the centre, so that the instrument could be retuned from B♭ to A. In 1847 the French maker F. Triébert also tried to construct a *clarinette multiphonique* which, like Simiot's instrument, could be retuned from C to B♭ and A by means of slides.

The construction of the above combination clarinets was fairly simple, even primitive, and the instruments are unlikely to have been very satisfactory in regard to purity of intonation. The relatively small extensions were probably insufficient to enable the player to play true notes in each of the different tunings. Recognising this, L. A. Buffet hit on an entirely new idea for the construction of combination clarinets. The instrument was patented in 1862 and consisted of two metal tubes, one inside the other. The outer tube carried the whole mechanism, which differed from an ordinary clarinet in that every ring and key affected two positions, namely the holes of A pitch and those of B♭ pitch. The inner tube had the same series of holes but arranged in such a way that in any position only one group of holes coincided with the corresponding group in the outer tube, while the others remained closed. A turn of the bell would alter the relative position of the holes and thus the pitch. According to Sachs (*Reallexikon*), the system found imitators in Austria. However, a British clarinettist James Clinton also took up Buffet's idea and was granted a German patent in 1891[1].

Italian makers also worked on the solution of the problem. A certain Rossi invented a combination clarinet in 1880 and the Milan firm of Maino and Orsi constructed a *clarinetto a doppia tonalità* in 1887, based on Simiot's original idea. A most interesting model was made in 1901 by the firm of Agostino Rampone of Milan at the

[1] Jacques Albert of Brussels built these Clinton instruments.

suggestion of the clarinettist Leoni of the same city, Based on the measurements of an A clarinet, this *clarino traspositore Si b= La* had a double complement of holes and keys for A and, about a quarter of an inch higher up, for B♭. The holes of one or the other series were closed by means of a special mechanism, so that the player was able to use exactly the same fingering for playing in A or B♭ according to which series of holes was open.

In the 1880s the firm of Berthold Brothers in Speyer made a rather awkward combination clarinet to designs by the Hamburg clarinettist Theodor Lässig, who took out a patent for it in 1889. The instrument consisted of a tube with two parallel bores but with one mouthpiece and one bell. According to the position of a valve, the air stream was conducted through one bore for A or through the other for B♭.

An extremely complicated instrument made by a Vienna dentist, the late Dr Loos, represents the latest attempt in this field. It was shown at the Frankfurt Musical Exhibition of 1927, patented in Austria in the same year and in Germany three years later.[1]

Modern clarinet systems

The desire further to improve the clarinet continues to worry musicians and makers at the present time. Some alterations to the key system and other innovations have been very successful, while others have been discarded or are still struggling for recognition. Only a few of the many inventions can be mentioned or described here and failure to mention any particular invention or inventor should not be taken to imply disapproval, any more than the detailed discussion of a particular model should necessarily be taken to imply approval.

The prototype of the German clarinet today is the well-known

[1] The 'double clarinet' in the Berlin instrument collection is not a combination clarinet. It represents the somewhat clumsy attempt of an unknown maker to construct a clarinet for playing in two parts. It has two very narrow mouthpieces and is actuated by two keyboards, each ranging over one and a half octaves. A very similar instrument may be seen in the Brussels collection.

and generally recognised model evolved by Oskar Oehler of Berlin on the basis of Ivan Müller's instrument. In the course of many years work, Oehler altered the position and shape of the keys and perfected the mechanism (figs. 10–12). Every instrument issuing from his workshop conforms to the highest standards in regard to tone and pitch; many makers today build clarinets to Oehler's model but few attain the same quality as the original.

The model Oskar Oehler finally evolved is so well-known to every clarinettist that a very brief description will suffice here. Oehler's instruments, all made to the same pattern, have 22 keys, five brille rings and one finger-plate: they are provided with the familiar forked $b''\flat$ mechanism, the so-called octave connection[1] on the back of the upper joint, the e''' improvement on the second brille ring, a $b'/c\sharp$ trill mechanism which can be disconnected if desired, and with one lever each for $e''\flat$, f'' and $g''\sharp$; in addition, they possess an ingenious forked f'' mechanism which works in such a way that when the player fingers the fork, the note is produced in exactly the same manner as by the normal keyed f'' and is therefore of the same quality and pitch.

Up to 1890 no improvement of the forked f'' was known. However, in the early 1890s the trade began to make available clarinets with a single forked f'' improvement, i.e. with only a single f'' vent key on the side. Oskar Oehler recognised the weakness of this invention, and, according to an account by F. A. Uebel, at a pub session one evening, probably about the turn of the century, he sketched a new fork mechanism on a beer mat.

This design provided for two keys on the side and a connecting lug from the lower of them to the $e''\flat$ key, and it was later executed in the workshop of Uebel's father. But Oehler was still not entirely satisfied and before the 1914–18 war introduced another improvement, omitting the connecting lug. As even this mechanism was not always reliable, F. Arthur Uebel of Markneukirchen, a pupil of Oehler, tried to improve it still further. The last remaining faults have happily been removed by means of a fresh connection with

---

[1] As this connecting rod from the speaker key to the top brille ring serves to improve the alternative fingering of $c''\sharp$, the name '$c''\sharp$ mechanism' would perhaps be more appropriate.

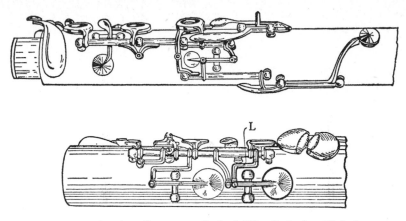

Top: Mechanism for a pure forked *f'* by F. Arthur Uebel
Bottom: Improvement of Oehler's forked *f"* mechanism by Arthur Uebel
(L=new lever)

independent springing. Instruments with this mechanism have been on the market since 1940.

Since 1941 the firm of F. A. Uebel has been making clarinets with a new mechanism for the production of a correctly-tuned forked *f'*. In this instrument the hole to be covered by the left index finger has been reduced in size to produce a pure note with the fork. A small key related to the upper joint brille, and the so-called octave connection automatically adjusts *c'''* which would otherwise sound too low. The *f'/c'''* key for the middle finger of the left hand is omitted in this instrument, although it can be provided if desired.

The clarinets designed by the solo clarinettist Ernst Schmidt, formerly of Mannheim, enjoy a good reputation. Schmidt proceeded from the assumption that the correct positioning of the holes was not an empirical matter but could be found only as a result of exact acoustic-mathematical calculations, and that the elimination of forked notes was desirable. His research, based on the work of Boehm, culminated in the 'Schmidt-Kolbe' clarinet which he produced in co-operation with the maker Louis Kolbe of Altenburg. The excessively large hole for the speaker key caused certain defects in pitch, since it was also used to produce *b'♭*, so that in 1912 the instrument was provided with a *b'♭* mechanism invented with the help of Kolbe. It consisted of a supplementary key for *b'♭* connected with the *a'* key or a half thumb-ring; in contrast to a similar mechanism on the bass clarinet, the speaker key also opens for *b'♭*. The bell which, in any case, serves decorative rather than acoustic purposes, was omitted, so that the lower end of this instrument is straight, as in a flute.

Ernst Schmidt's 'Reform [modified] Boehm clarinet' (fig. 12) is based on the same principles as the Schmidt-Kolbe clarinet, except that the *c"* and *e"♭* as well as the *b'* and *c"♯* keys for the little fingers of the right and the left hand respectively are provided with rollers just as in instruments of the 'German' system, without any changes to the shapes required by the 'Boehm fingering' and despite the presence of the alternative keys below.[1]

After his retirement Ernst Schmidt took another great step forward in the perfection of his life's work through his friendship and co-operation with the clarinet-playing physicist Friedrich Rösch of Heidelberg. Schmidt and Rösch thoroughly examined the acoustic principles of the clarinet and, with the aid of diagrams and formulas, made an exact calculation of the measurements for the Schmidt clarinets built by Fritz Wurlitzer. Not content with this, they also investigated the measurements of the largest and smallest types.

The firm of J. Mollenhauer and Sons of Fulda conducted an interesting experiment in the 1860s when it manufactured a clarinet based on the strictest application of Boehm's principles. The toneholes of this instrument were adjusted in accordance with exact calculations and were served by a complicated mechanism of independent plates and keys, so that no hole was covered directly by a finger. The model received a prize at the Paris World Exhibition of 1867 and in addition, at the suggestion of the clarinettist A. Romero already mentioned, a special recognition by the Spanish Government. However, in practice the instrument apparently did not come up to expectation.

[1] Today the firm of Wurlitzer, Bubenreuth and Erlbach/Vogtland, makes Schmidt-Kolbe and Reform Boehm clarinets. Wurlitzer also makes very good bass clarinets descending to low *c*, with special forked *f"* and a *c'♯–g"♯* mechanism, which make feasible the slur from *b'* or *c"♯* to *g"♯* (unsatisfactory in the Oehler clarinet) and a perfect *f"♯–g"♯* trill.

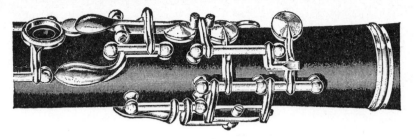

Patent *b'♭* mechanism by Georg Grässel

The 'German Normal Clarinet' was more successful. It was developed in 1890 by Th. Mollenhauer in close co-operation with the clarinettist Hermann Kunze of Elberfeld. The instrument represents an attempt to combine the Buffet-Klosé system with that of Ivan Müller. Of the latter it retained the old fingering for *b/f"♯* and *f'♯/c'"♯*, and of the former the disposition of the group of keys for the little finger of the right hand. In addition, the clarinet had an *f"♯/g"♯* trill mechanism and a connection permitting the opening of the *e'♭/b"♭* and *f'/c'"* keys by the depression of any one ring. Later the same firm made the 'Union clarinet', which likewise retained 'German' fingering but included the Boehm system's alternative keys for the little fingers.

For some time, the 'Normal Patent Clarinet' by Wilhelm Heckel of Biebrich-am-Rhein was popular. The main advantage of the instrument lay in the division of the thumb-key into a speaker and a *b'♭* key. Moreover, Heckel's clarinet had a 'Reform' mouthpiece which guaranteed a purer tone; the vent keys provided for a time were meant to serve the same purpose.

Georg Grässel (today, Fritz Grässel) of Nuremberg, a former collaborator of Oskar Oehler, built clarinets to his own specifications (protected by patent from 1919). The instruments possess a novel mechanism for the production of pure *a/e"*, forked *b♭/f"*, *e'♭/b"♭* and forked *f'/c'"*; they have an *f"♯/g"♯* and the normal *b'/c"♯* trill as well as a 'patent B♭ mechanism' (automatic separate *b'♭* and speaker keys), intended to produce a clear *b'♭* and *b'* and a true *e*. In addition, the Grässel clarinets have an appropriate mechanism to facilitate the slurs *b'/g"♯* and *c"♯/g"♯*.

The separation of the *b'♭* and speaker keys is indispensable in the deep clarinets and desirable in the normal instrument. If the *b'♭* hole serves also as an overblowing hole, the tones *b'* and *c"* tend to sound a little sharp. If these notes are pitched correctly, *e* and *f* sound too low. This tendency can be corrected by means of an *e* vent key on the bell, actuated by the right thumb. The *f*, also too low, can only be corrected by a second key connected with the thumb lever and closing automatically when low *e* is fingered. This last improvement has recently been adopted by the firm of Uebel and others (e.g. Müller of Bremen).

Another popular instrument, patented in 1934, is the clarinet made by the Leipzig chamber musician Hans Berninger and the maker Clemens Wurlitzer of Wernitzgrün. Its automatic auxiliary keys for the Oehler as well as for the Boehm system are meant to produce a truer tuning and an improvement on the somewhat unpleasing tone of *b'♭*. The inventors based their refinement on the experience familiar to all clarinettists that the notes from *e* to *g♯* and from *e"* to *a"* tend to sound too flat, while from *a* to *d'* are too sharp. To correct this fault, they provided vent keys actuated by the speaker key. The improvement of *b'♭* is brought about by a new fingering device, i.e. the simultaneous opening of the *a'* and the third trill key for the right index finger, which by means of a new connection, may also be opened by the left thumb.[1] According to a very favourable opinion by the Leipzig clarinettist Professor Edmund Heyneck, the inventors have succeeded in removing the tuning defects of the clarinet.

With the appearance of so many jazz bands in which the saxophonist has to play the clarinet as well, 'clarinets with saxophone fingering' came on the market, and they are still on offer in the catalogues of some firms. Like any other clarinet, these instruments overblow a twelfth and not, like a saxophone, an octave, so that it is hardly accurate to speak of saxophone fingering. The promising name is earned merely by the fact that in these clarinets all fingerholes have been replaced by plates and that the notes *b♭/f"* and

---

[1] Instead of this lever connection, Wurlitzer occasionally supplies a *b'♭* key, taking the exact position of the third trill key. Manipulated simultaneously, this *b'♭*, the *a'* and the speaker keys produce a true *b'*.

b/f"♯ are fingered according to the French (Boehm) system as on the saxophone.

Clarinets have indeed been constructed which appear to overblow to the octave. In fact, these instruments still overblow a twelfth but, on account of an extremely complicated key system, the fingering remains the same for every octave. Clarinets of this kind have been made by T. Valand of Egersund, Norway, and Georgy Carnock and Antonin Konrád of Prague. The latter were granted a Czech patent in 1930 and a German one in 1932.

There have been many other attempts to improve the clarinet by ingenious technicians and musicians. Among inventors aiming at a complete renovation of the instrument and its mechanism were Dr Shohe Tanaka of Japan; Allen Loomis of Toledo, Ohio; John William McAvoy of Bangor, North Wales; Max Zacherl of Landshut, Bavaria; and Fritz Stein of Saarbrücken. The thermos clarinet by the American W. S. Haynes should be mentioned here; it is supposed to warm up rapidly and evenly. In some cases it is too early as yet to give a final verdict on the practical value of these instruments but it does not appear as though any of them will be successful in the long run.

Special clarinets were constructed for the purpose of playing the compositions of the quarter-tone composers, long since forgotten. The first to tackle the problem was the musicologist Dr R. H. Stein of Berlin, himself a clarinettist. He designed a quarter-tone clarinet in 1911 which was built a year later by the firm of V. Kohlert and Sons in Graslitz. Dr Stein had conceived an instrument which differed from a normal B♭ clarinet only in having additional quarter-tone keys, but in 1933 the maker Fritz Schüller of Markneukirchen took out a patent for a two-tube quarter-tone clarinet (fig. 13). The instrument had a switch-valve below the mouthpiece by means of which the air stream could be conducted either through a tube producing normal B♭ pitch or into a slightly longer tube pitched a quarter-tone lower. The mechanism functions in such a way that keys and plates serve both bores simultaneously.

The introduction of the clarinet

Although the transformation of the chalumeau into the clarinet occurred about 1700, the new instrument was rarely used in the first half of the eighteenth century and gained general recognition only from about 1750 onwards. L. de Burbure mentions as the earliest score containing clarinet passages a Mass composed about 1720 by the organist of Antwerp Cathedral, J. A. J. Faber.[1]

According to Rudolf Wagner, who did some research in the matter, four clarinets of boxwood (the most popular material until the nineteenth century) were purchased in 1712 on behalf of the Nuremberg municipal music (*Ratsmusik*).

The 1716 catalogue of the Amsterdam publishers Roger et Le Cène offered some anonymous compositions and Airs for two clarinets composed by Dreux. Some of the anonymous works have been republished by Dr Heinz Becker (Breitkopf & Härtel, Wiesbaden, 1954, Coll. Mus., no. 106), whose volume also contains Duets by Rousseau and Carl Philipp Emanuel Bach and was published under the title of *Klarinettenduette aus der Frühzeit des Instrumentes*. The early anonymous pieces are little fanfares in D not written specifically for the clarinet, for, as the title indicated, they could be played by two chalumeaux, trumpets, horns, oboes, flutes or violins; the original title runs '*Airs à deux Chalumeaux, deux Trom-*

[1] It might be assumed that this clarinet part was meant for a high solo trumpet. But Burbure quotes an example from the score which shows the clarinet-like character of the part in question. Unfortunately, it has not been possible to inspect the original score which, according to information kindly supplied by M. Pols, archivist of Antwerp, has disappeared. The solo alto voice is accompanied by two flutes, C clarinet and continuo. The clarinet is taken in chordal figuration down to low *f*, then the lowest note possible.

pettes, deux Hautbois, deux Violins, deux Flûtes, deux Clarinelles ou Cors de Chasse'. *'Clarinelles'* is obviously a printer's error. The catalogue has *'Clarinettes'*. Rendered on high clarinets, preferably two D (or Eb) clarinets playing in C major, the little pieces are quite charming, although they are not very suitable for normal clarinets.

As shown by Werner Menke, Telemann, in his Cantata for Whitsunday, composed in 1721, specified a clarinet (a soprano aria is to be accompanied by 'Flauto piccolo, Clarinetto et Quartett'). Pincherle and Kolneder found that Vivaldi also used the clarinet; the pieces are contained in the new edition of the complete works of Vivaldi, published by Ricordi. There is a Concerto in C major for two oboes, two clarinets (in C), strings and harpsichord (F.XII, No. 1); another Concerto in the same key and for the same instruments (with a *Largo* middle movement for the four solo wind instruments only, F.XII, No. 2); and a Concerto in C major *per la Solennità di S. Lorenzo* (for the festival of St Laurence) for two flutes, two oboes, two clarinets, bassoon, two solo violins, strings and harpsichord (F.XII, No. 14, all three concertos edited by A. Ephrikian). In some instances the clarinets are still treated in a trumpet manner but various passages show that they cannot have been intended for natural trumpets (*clarini*). Performance on modern instruments (preferably good C clarinets) demands a very precise tone-delivery, lest in comparison with the oboes, the clarinets sound vulgar and ridiculous, since our modern instruments no longer possess the much harder, sharper sound of the early clarinets.

There is some evidence for a very early use of clarinets in Kremsmünster Abbey. When the master of the Abbey music, Nonnos Stadler, retired in 1747 he caused an inventory to be made, which lists amongst other instruments 'two boxwood clarinets' which had been at the Abbey before his appointment in 1739. According to the *Frankfurter Frag- und Anzeigungs-Nachrichten*, two clarinettists[1] performed in Frankfurt-am-Main in 1739, and 10 years later the clarinet was used in an Oratorio by the music director Beck.

As early as 1741 an inventory of the court orchestra of Sayn-

---

[1] 'Advertisement. Two good clarinettists have arrived at the Windmill in All Saints Lane; anyone wishing to hear them perform will be welcome.'

Wittgenstein lists two pairs of clarinets, and 1732 the Mainz court orchestra engaged a clarinettist.

In 1755 two clarinettists (Wack and Engel) are mentioned for the first time in the budget of an orchestra (Thurn and Taxis court orchestra, Regensburg), although previously some musicians, mostly flautists and oboists, had played the clarinet as a second instrument.

In 1742 a Hungarian virtuoso performed in Dublin in concertos for clarinet, 'shalamo' (chalumeau) and other wind instruments. London first heard the clarinet probably not before 1751, at a concert given in the Haymarket Theatre, and then repeatedly in the following years, e.g. 1754, 1756, 1763. Examples of J. C. Bach's use of the clarinet include *L'Olimpe*, 1753; *Orione*, performed in London in 1763; and the 'wind symphonies' (for two clarinets, two horns and one or two bassoons). (For further information about the introduction of the clarinet in Britain, see Rendall.)

There is not quite such early evidence for the use of the clarinet in France. The great *Encyclopédie* of 35 volumes (see p. 22) mentions it but has a description of the instrument only in the supplementary volume of 1776. In 1749 Rameau used two clarinets in his opera *Zoroastre*, and among the instrumentalists in the 1751 performance of his Pastorale *Acanthe et Céphise* we find the names of four clarinet-tists.[1] In the spring of 1755 a Symphony for clarinets and horns by Johann Stamitz was performed in Paris as one of the *Concerts spirituels* and from then on clarinettists could be heard fairly frequently in these concerts. Although no symphony with original parts for the clarinet[2] by J. Stamitz has been preserved, it may be assumed that clarinets took over or reinforced the oboe parts, for many works of that period and the succeeding years contained directions to the effect that oboes might be replaced by clarinets

[1] Mennicke claims, however, that the clarinet parts in *Acanthe* were really intended for the clarino and show a typical trumpet character; he quotes some evidence designed to prove Rameau's ignorance of the clarinet. In answer to an enquiry by the present author, L. de la Laurencie, who has made a special study of the problem, has effectively refuted all Mennicke's arguments. The subject is discussed in detail by Brenet (Rameau), Cucuel, la Laurencie, Mennicke, and Prod'homme.

[2] According to Boese, the Schlossbibliothek in Berlin has several copies of a symphony by J. Stamitz in which, in one edition, the original oboe parts are transposed for B♭ clarinets.

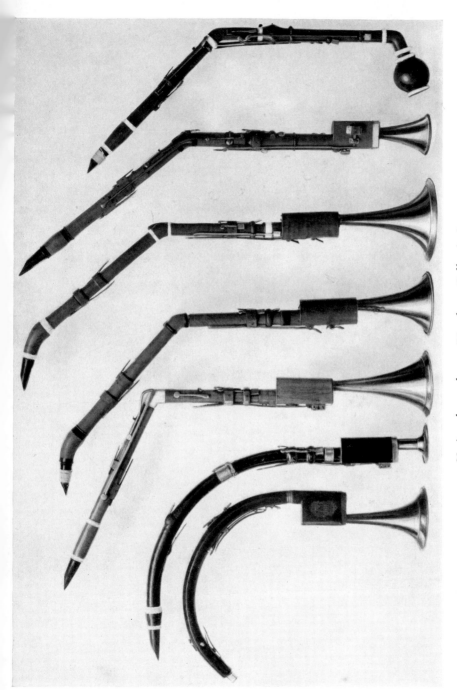

15 *Various basset horns (Hamburg Collection)*

16 Clarinette d'amour (Hamburg Collection)   17a, b Back and front of a modern basset horn by Arthur Uebel, Markneukirchen. At the back, the four Basset keys for low *c* to *e♮*

or vice versa. The Leipzig *Allgemeine Musikalische Zeitung* of 1802 writes about this custom: 'In France (where people tend to go to extremes) the clarinet, instead of the oboe, is in almost general use for symphonies', and Backofen also reports: 'Among the wind instruments, the clarinet is still the favourite of the French and that to such a degree that in symphonies and concertos where the clarinet is not expressly specified, they make it take over the oboe parts.'[1]

At that time, the clarinet was introduced into French military music and there also ousted the oboe from its leading position. Most clarinettists in France and Belgium were of German origin, and for many decades German players also performed in the big Paris orchestras. Even in Berlioz's time, French players could not stand comparison with the Germans, so that the composer expressed the opinion that the lungs of French musicians were perhaps not as strong as those of the Germans. The first theoretical work about the use of the clarinet, Valentin Roeser's *Essai d'instruction à l'usage de ceux qui composent pour la clarinette et le cor* (1764), was published in Paris. A unique copy is in the Royal Library, Brussels.

The clarinet made a fairly early appearance in the St Petersburg orchestra where it was mentioned by Hiller in 1759. The new instrument soon became a favourite among amateur musicians there. For instance, in 1764 the 'Polish count and knight' Oginski and the court musician Lankammer performed virtuoso compositions for two clarinets with their own orchestra. According to the diary of Count K. von Zinzendorf, Oginski played his own compositions for the clarinet in 1761 at the Vienna residence of Duke Esterhazy.

A very strange remark is contained in the autobiography of Benjamin Franklin where he states that he heard the clarinet being played in Bethlehem, Pennsylvania, in 1756. As he did not write down his reminiscences until 1788, it is just possible that his memory was at fault, for the clarinet is most unlikely to have been known in a small American town at a time when it had not been adopted even by the largest orchestras in Europe.

The earliest known concertos for clarinet were composed by

---

[1] In Italian orchestras there was sometimes no oboe at all and its part was given to the clarinet.

Kapellmeister Johann Melchior Molter of Durlach (*c.* 1695–1765). Although they are referred to in Eitner's *Quellenlexikon*, they remained otherwise practically unknown. After Rendall had drawn attention to two of the four concertos, Heinz Becker examined the compositions in detail (*Die Musikforschung*, VIII, 1955, pp. 286 ff.) and re-edited the four concertos (together with two clarinet concertos by Franz Xaver Pokorny), in *Erbe deutscher Musik*, vol. 41, 1957 (see its preface). Becker believes that they date from between 1740 and 1750.

Molter's concertos are all intended for the D clarinet. The solo part is treated in clarino manner, and below the written *c"* (sounding *d"*) one meets a purely triadic theme. The clarinet moves chiefly in the high and highest registers (not uncommonly up to written *g'''*). In theory these concertos can be executed on the clarino; some virtuosi have been known to reach such extreme heights. But Becker feels justified in excluding this possibility by a comparison with a genuine Clarino Concerto by Molter. (A clarino is a natural trumpet, normally in D, on which the high trumpet parts were executed. As the instrument was capable of producing only the natural harmonies, it had to have a much longer tube than the modern valve trumpet in order to produce a scale in the octave *c"–c'''*. Replicas of these instruments are made by H. Finke of Herford and used by the Capella Coloniensis and others. Denner probably believed that with the 'clarinetto' (small clarino) he had provided a substitute for the clarino, which was difficult to play. There can be no doubt that the early clarinets, mostly in the keys of D or C, had a more trumpet-like sound than modern instruments.)

With the clear sound of the D clarinets and with their still almost baroque way of treatment, the Molter concertos have great charm, though because of the sustained high register they are exacting to play and a performance should not be undertaken by any but experienced players of small clarinets. They were probably composed for Johann Reusch who worked in Durlach as a flautist but also played oboe and clarinet. Such facts (more details are to be found in Becker's work) indicate that the clarinet was not introduced into the orchestra for the first time by the Mannheimers, as is often stated.

Probably the oldest picture of a clarinettist is to be found in Weigl's *Musikalisches Theatrum* (*c.* 1740; facsimile reproduction by Bärenreiter, 1961, in the series *Documenta Musicologia*). The picture shows a room with an elegantly dressed gentleman playing the clarinet. The caption runs:

Clarinet

When the trumpet call is all too loud,
The clarinet does serve to please
Eschewing both the high and lowest sound,
It varies gracefully and thus attains the prize.
Wherefore the noble spirit, enamoured of this reed,
Instruction craves and plays assiduously.

It is interesting to note that here too the sound of the clarinet is set against that of the trumpet.

Meanwhile, the clarinet made further progress. It was now quite often possible to hear itinerant virtuosi and to find prominent orchestras employing clarinettists. Thus, from 1758 or 1759 onwards the famous Mannheim Orchestra always had two instrumentalists playing the clarinet. There is evidence to show that in 1764 there were clarinettists at Wallerstein, where Philipp Carl, on the occasion of a visit from Emperor Francis I, had 'French horns and clarinets' play at table. However, it is possible that these musicians played the clarinet only occasionally or were visitors to the residence, for there is proof of a full-time clarinettist only from 1778 onwards. The orchestra of the Bishop of Grosswardein had a '*Konzertspieler* of the clarinet' already in 1765 under the directorship of Dittersdorf. The latter mentions the presence of a clarinettist as early as 1754 at Schlosshof/March, a summer residence of the Prince of Hildburghausen. In 1766 the orchestra of the Prince of Prussia in Berlin counted two clarinettists among its members, and the court orchestra of Passau employed a 'Chief tower-musician, also a reserve flautist and clarinet virtuoso' from 1762 to 1767. Clarinettists proper arrived in Passau only in 1786, although in the period between 1763 and 1774 there were 'two ordinary and one solo clarinet' among the instruments.

Gradually court and private orchestras began to employ clarinettists, and in the 1780s and 90s they were to be found in most orchestras. The Vienna court orchestra employed the brothers Stadler as

Portrait of a clarinettist from Weigl's *Musikalisches Theatrum* (c. 1740)

clarinettists in 1787;[1] Dresden followed suit in 1794 but in the pre-
ceeding years had been borrowing clarinettists from the military
band. The Leipzig Gewandhaus Orchestra already had its clarinettist in 1784.

An interesting reason was put forward for the appointment of a
clarinettist in Dresden. In the first place, it was considered that
service in the military band as well as in the court orchestra was
too strenuous for a musician (two had died of tuberculosis!), and
the argument continued: 'At the present time, the local orchestra
is probably the only one which, in spite of its superiority in other
respects, still lacks a clarinet and basset horn, instruments which
are constantly being demanded by modern composers. It is impossible to make any progress with more recent compositions
unless these instruments are played by artists of the same excellence
as the other members of the orchestra and are put on the same
footing with the others.'

Fifteen years previously, J. A. Hiller had noted as a particular
rarity that J. F. Agricola included parts for the clarinet in his opera
Amore e Psiche (1767). Hiller wrote in this connection: 'Any
sensible composer knows how to go with the times and there can
be no doubt that this penetrating and powerful instrument could
well hold its place among wind instruments if it were played by
skilful people and with some zeal; but so far it has served only to
render the sound of the fife more warlike and the sound of the
drum more bearable.' In 1788 Hiller included four clarinets in his
performance of Handel's *Messiah* in Breslau.[2]

The reasons for the addition of the clarinet to the community of
orchestral instruments and its popularity as a solo instrument are
no doubt to be found partly in its improved tone and technique,
but above all in the change in ideals of sonority which was taking

[1] In 1781 the Vienna military band consisted of two shawms (wide-bore oboes), two
clarinets, two French horns, one trumpet, small and large drums (Nicolai, *Beschreibung
einer Reise . . . im Jahre 1781*, Berlin and Stettin, 1784, IV, 558).

[2] Handel composed an *Ouverture* for two clarinets (in D) and horn (Fitzwilliam
Museum, Cambridge). It was published (for Bb clarinets) by Schott & Co., London. See
also R. B. Chatwin, 'Handel and the Clarinet', *Galpin Society Journal*, 1950. According to
that publication, the two *cornetti* originally specified in the undated Granville score of
Tamerlano were replaced by *clar. 1°* and *clar. 2°*, presumably signifying clarinets. In
Riccardo Primo (1727) Handel used chalumeaux.

place at that time. While the matter-of-fact tone of the oboe corresponded with musical sensibilities in the baroque period and the flute became the symbol, as it were, of the rococo, the clarinet gave expression to the era of the sentimental and romanticism. D. Schubart enthusiastically described the warm, sensual sound of the clarinet in the following terms: 'Its character symbolises the melting sentiments of love—it is the tone of the passionate heart ... The tone is so mellifluous, so languishing; and he who knows how to bring out the medium timbre, is sure to conquer every heart.'

In his later years, Carl Philipp Emanuel Bach showed a definite preference for the clarinet. He did not use it in his Berlin compositions though he probably came to know the instrument while employed at the court of Frederick the Great. He did not use it in compositions until after he had taken Telemann's place in Hamburg, where it is likely that he frequently had occasion to hear visiting virtuosi. He was especially fond of including parts for two clarinets in his little pieces, marches and sonatas for five and seven wind instruments (Wtq. 184, 185, 186), as also in minuets and polonaises (Wtq. 189, 190). As a solo instrument, he used it in the two-movement Duet for clarinets (Wtq. 142) and in the six sonatas for clarinet, bassoon and harpsichord (Wtq. 92), enchanting little single-movement pieces. The clarinet parts of the Duet would have presented no special difficulties to contemporary players but those of the Trio, in parts at least, demanded virtuosi. Regardless of technical difficulties, Bach here writes in the high register—up to f'''—a feat which 20 years later Mozart dared not call for, even in his Clarinet Concerto (as he wrote it). It is surprising how little use was made of the low register of the clarinet; the part moves mostly in the register from b' upwards and never goes lower than b, though in the duet the clarinet parts occasionally descend to g and in the clarinet Sonatas even to f (Wtq. 184).

The sonatas (Wtq. 92) for clarinet, bassoon and harpsichord were published in 1955 by the International Music Company, New York. The duet for two clarinets is contained in Nagel's Musical Archives, No. 35, and also in the volume *Klarinettenduette aus der Frühzeit des Instrumentes* already mentioned. The same volume also contains four airs for two clarinets by the philosopher Jean-Jacques Rousseau.

They are short, melodious, simple pieces, though of doubtful value as compositions.

Among the earliest clarinet concertos are two by Franz Xaver Pokorny. Both originated about 1765 at the court of Oettingen-Wallerstein. The E♭ major Concerto was scored '*per il Clarinetto primo*' (compass of the solo part, *c'–e'''*), the B♭ major Concerto '*per il Clarinetto secundo*' (compass, *f–c'''*). First clarinettists apparently preferred the higher register (as among brass players to this day) and the second players more the lower. The concertos were intended for the B♭ clarinet and, unlike Molter's concertos, the B♭ major Concerto makes full use of the low register. They are contained in volume 41, mentioned above (p. 50), of *Erbe deutscher Musik* (edited by Heinz Becker and also available in pianoforte arrangement with solo part), though they are interesting mainly for study purposes.

The clarinet in the works of the Mannheim and Vienna composers of the eighteenth century

As has been pointed out, the Mannheimers were not solely responsible for the introduction of the clarinet but the Mannheim court orchestra played a decisive part in the general adoption of the instrument. Certainly from 1758 onwards there were two clarinettists in the orchestra. Peter Gradenwitz, the most eminent Johann Stamitz scholar of the present day, discovered in the Thurn and Taxis court library in Regensburg a Clarinet Concerto which he ascribes to the famous leader of the Mannheim court orchestra, Johann Stamitz (1717–1757). If his judgement is to be accepted, this would be one of the earliest known clarinet concertos—apart from those by Molter. The work was edited in 1953 by Gradenwitz and published by the Leeds Music Corporation, New York. It is scored for the B♭ clarinet, in B♭ major with string accompaniment. Musically speaking, the piece is of much better quality than the many concertos by the composer's son, Karl Stamitz (1745–1801), who was a famous virtuoso on the viola d'amore. We know at least

11 of the latter's clarinet concertos and two double concertos, one for two clarinets and one for clarinet and bassoon. One or two of these works may have been written in collaboration with the clarinettist Joseph Beer. Available are the four solo concertos (B♭ major, No. 3; E♭ major, No. 9; B♭ major, No. 10; and the *Darmstadt Concerto* in E♭ major, No. 1; also, the Double Concerto with bassoon).

Karl Stamitz uses the clarinet chiefly as a singing instrument and in most cases prefers an expressive melodiousness to virtuosity. He makes no great technical demands on the player, although the virtuoso had every chance in the free cadenza to show the full range of his skill. The upper limit of the solo part mostly lies in d''' and e''', with the cadenzas—probably only in rare instances written by the composer—in f''' and g'''. Stamitz used the low register, as Faber did before him in his Mass of 1720, preferably for chordal figures. He utilised the juxtaposition of the registers—especially effective with the clarinet—by great leaps in the melodic arc of the clarinet and by the repetition in the high register of a passage first played in the low one.

Concerto ex Dis (E♭), first movement ('Darmstadt Concerto')

There were other composers of the Mannheim school who took pains with the clarinet concerto, though not quite to the same extent as Karl Stamitz. A Concerto by Ernst Eichner which is still extant, proved to be a transposition of his Oboe Concerto of 1772. Dimler composed a concerto, probably in the last decade of the eighteenth century, for his son then working in Munich, which shows the author's intimate knowledge of Mozart's style. Another concerto of the same period was composed by the clarinettist Georg Friedrich Fuchs, who spent most of his working life in Paris. Its last movement allows the virtuoso to develop the full range of his superior technique. Among later composers of the Mannheim school, some of whom wrote brilliant concertos for the clarinet, were Franz Tausch, Peter von Winter and Franz Danzi. Winter also wrote a Double Concerto for clarinet and cello (for Baermann and Legrand).

The concertos of the clarinettist Franz Tausch, teacher of Heinrich Baermann, are brilliant pieces of composition, full of daring passages and leaps and it is extremely surprising that contemporary clarinettists were able to master them on their technically not as yet very highly developed instruments. In one cadenza Tausch takes the clarinet to *c''''*! Technically Tausch made greater demands even than Weber and Spohr in their later concertos.

etc. chromatically to

F. Tausch, Clarinet Concerto in E♭ major, No. 2, first movement, bars 154 ff.

The 'Mannheimers' already composed chamber music as well for the clarinet. There are three quartet sets by Karl Stamitz for clarinet, violin, viola and cello, although in the Quartets Opus 4 the clarinet is mentioned only as a substitute for the first violin. However, in Opus 8 it takes the leading part and is specified as the first instrument, to be replaced only in an emergency by some other woodwind; and in the concertante Quartets Opus 12 the clarinet is employed in such a characteristic manner that it can hardly be replaced, in spite of a remark on the title page to the effect that the violin could take its place. Franz Tausch also wrote a quartet (printed in 1822) for the same instruments, and so did Peter von Winter, in addition to a septet and an octet with clarinet. Four of Stamitz's quartets are in print today, and the Sonata concertante in B♭ major (first edition, 1818) for clarinet and piano by Franz Danzi (1763–1826) has recently been republished (by Simrock, 1960, edited by Wojciechowski). This is all the more welcome because few original contemporary pieces for these two instruments are available, although relatively many solo concertos have been published in recent years. Mention should be made of the charming and technically undemanding Sonata in B♭ major by Jan Vanhal (or Johann Baptist Wanhal, 1739–1813, who also wrote trios for clarinet, violin and figured bass), published in 1948 by McGinnis & Marx, New York. Unlike the masterly, almost concerto-like Danzi Sonata, Vanhal's Sonata was not written specifically for the clarinet; *c′* is the lowest note and the original title was *Sonata per il clavicembalo o pianoforte con clarinetto o violino obligato.*

We do not know when and how the clarinet first appeared in Vienna. It was not included in the court orchestra until 1787, although clarinettists had been playing in Vienna considerably earlier. It is safe to assume that the clarinet did not finally take hold in the imperial city until 1770, even though an occasional player may have been heard there previously.

Burney states in his *The Present State of Music in Germany* ... (1773): 'There was music every day, during dinner, and in the evening at the inn, where I lodged [in 1772], which was the Golden Ox; but it was usually bad, particularly that of a band of wind instruments, which constantly attended the ordinary. This consisted of French horns, clarinets, hautboys, and bassoons. . . .'

In his operas *Orfeo* (1762) and *Alceste* (1767), composed specifically for Vienna, Gluck was still content with the primitive chalumeau, and switched to clarinets only in the later arrangements of these works for performance in Paris (1774 and 1776) and in *Iphigénie en Aulide* (1774). In the latter work, the clarinet appears only occasionally, more frequently in the Paris *Orphée*, and in the *Alceste* score almost constantly. However, it should be noted that in almost every case Gluck used the clarinet in conjunction with oboes, violins, flutes or horns, and very rarely as a solo instrument. He barely utilised its full compass; for example, the entire clarinet part in *Orphée* lies within the *a–e‴* scale, and the highest and lowest notes of even that range occur very infrequently indeed.

Joseph Haydn employed the clarinet much earlier than Gluck, as he had one at his disposal during his work in Lukaveč near Pilsen (1759–1761) in the orchestra of Duke Morzin.

Haydn left no solo works for the clarinet. In his symphonies he used it comparatively late but always in character (No. 99 in E♭; No. 100 in G, 'The Military', in the second movement; No. 103 in E♭ 'With the drum roll'). To some others, clarinet parts have been added subsequently (e.g. No. 101, 'The Clock', in D major). In the late oratorios the clarinet was given an effective role. Some of Haydn's many *Feldharmonien* and divertimentos include the clarinet, among them the most charming little Divertimento in C major (Hoboken II: 14) for two C clarinets and two horns in low C (Haydn's complete works for wind instruments have been published by Doblinger, edited by Robbins Landon). Of Haydn's contemporaries in Vienna besides Mozart and other younger composers, Wenzel Pichl had a predilection for the clarinet and composed several concertos for it.

W. A. Mozart had a fleeting acquaintance with the clarinet at an early age. Perhaps he first heard it as early as 1763 at an 'academy' of the Mannheim orchestra in Schwetzingen, or perhaps not before 1764 in London. He certainly learned something of its technique when he copied C. F. Abel's Symphony Opus VII/6, which for many years was believed to be a brilliant work (K.18) of the child prodigy. Mozart first employed clarinets in 1771 in the Divertimento (K.113) for the private orchestra of a patron in Milan. The Divertimentos of 1773 (K.166 and 186) already show a much more skilful use mostly of two clarinets; by combining oboes and clarinets, Mozart here contrives a number of beautiful combinations of tone-colour.

We do not know whether, in the meantime, Mozart had gained some more intimate knowledge of the clarinet. On his journey to Paris in 1777–78 he certainly had ample opportunity, first in Munich[1] and later especially in Mannheim, to study the capabilities of the instrument. 'Alas, if only we also had clarinets', he wrote in a letter to his father.[2] 'You cannot imagine the wonderful effect of a symphony with flutes, oboes and clarinets.' It is all the more surprising that in the symphony (K.297) composed in Paris he used the clarinet only sparingly. The Sinfonia Concertante for oboe,

[1] 4 November 1777.
[2] 3 December 1778.

clarinet, horn and bassoon is probably not in this form attributable to Mozart. It may be an arrangement of a lost Sinfonia Concertante by him for flute, oboe, clarinet and horn. Another work which should be mentioned here is the Piano Quintet in E♭ (K.452), with oboes, clarinet, horn and bassoon, though here the leading part is given to the oboe.

From this time onwards, Mozart used the clarinet more frequently. With the basset horn, it was his favourite instrument. His opera scores include the clarinet from *Idomeneo* (1780), and 'in the typically German manner, later adopted by Beethoven and Weber, he employs it to express longing' (Komorzynski). In *Così fan tutte* the sound of the clarinet becomes 'the expressive interpreter of lovers, while the nasal utterance of the oboe usually accompanies the sarcasms of the old buffoon Alfonso' (Paumgartner, *Instrumentation*). It is interesting to note that Mozart always used the sound of the clarinet with great economy, saving it for particularly moving and soulful parts. In the *Die Entführung* the clarinet is to be heard in Belmonte's first aria 'Hier soll ich dich denn sehen', where it accompanies the voice. It does not occur again until Constanze's aria 'Ach, ich liebte', with parallel thirds. It is of no significance in the following trio and is completely omitted until the great Constanze aria 'Martern aller Arten'. (The aria which precedes this, usually omitted, is accompanied by the basset horn.) Apart from the unimportant clarinet part in the drinking duet, the instrument comes into its own in Belmonte's arias 'Wenn der Freude Tränen fliessen' and 'Ich baue ganz auf deine Stärke' and in Belmonte's and Constanze's duet 'Welch ein Geschick'. A similar trend is to be found in *Figaro*. The clarinet does not occur in any of the first five numbers until Cherubino's aria 'Non sò più cosa son', and throughout the rest of the opera takes part only in especially intimate and sensuous passages. The wonderfully soft opening of its part in the E♭ major Larghetto of the last finale is typical and most effective.

Mozart's first chamber works with the clarinet were written for Jaquin's circle of friends. The series began (between 1783 and 1785) with the five enchanting Divertimentos for two clarinets or basset horns and bassoon (K.439b, formerly appendix 229), published in

1813 by Simrock in a quintet arrangement with two additional French horns. The original probably specified three basset horns (see also M. Whewell, 'Mozart's Bassethorn Trios', *Musical Times*, London, vol. 103, January 1962). In a letter dated 31 May 1800, Konstanze Mozart wrote to André: 'Stadler had got copies of some unpublished Trios for basset horns. He claims that the baggage containing these things was stolen in Germany'. The compositions referred to may have been these Divertimentos. In 1786 Mozart composed the wonderful 'Kegelstatt Trio' (K.498) with viola and piano, so-called because this 'magical piece of smiling melancholy and sweet tunefulness' (Paumgartner, *Mozart*) is believed to have been written in the middle of the noisy chatter of a game of skittles.[1] In 1789 Mozart wrote the Quintet (K.581) for his friend Anton Stadler. With its expressive melody and heavenly harmonies, it became the ideal aspired to by many later composers, and the imperishable heritage of every clarinettist. The Clarinet Concerto (K.622) written in the year of Mozart's death (1789) was also for Stadler and originally conceived for the basset horn, an instrument of which Stadler was an unsurpassed virtuoso, as shown by a draft score for the first movement. This work also revels in the rich capabilities offered by the instrument and is an immortal gem of clarinet music.[2]

The original manuscripts of the Concerto and the Quintet are no longer extant. It has been suspected for some time that both compositions were originally written for Stadler's 'bass clarinet', an instrument which, like the basset horn, comprises written *c* [see also George Dazeley in *The Music Review*, IX, p. 169; Jiri Kratochvil, 'Betrachtungen über die Urfassung des Konzerts für Klarinette und des Quintets für Klarinette und Streicher von W. A. Mozart', in *Kongressbericht der Internationalen Konferenz über das Leben und Werk Mozarts*, Prague, May 1956; Jiri Kratochvil, 'Ist die heute gebräuchliche Fassung des Klarinettenkonzerts und des Klarinettenquintetts

---

[1] It should be pointed out that the duets for two clarinets (published by C. F. Schmidt), much used in music lessons and played by amateurs, are not original works by Mozart but rather free arrangements of Mozart's piano and violin compositions by André or one of his associates.

[2] Busoni and Ibert composed large-scale cadenzas to the second movement of the Concerto.

authentisch?', in *Beiträge zur Musikwissenschaft*, 1960, pp. 27–43].
This instrument, which must have existed in A and B♭, is described
today (following Kratochvil) as a basset clarinet, since what is
commonly called a 'bass clarinet' is a different instrument. Stadler
is known to have made such instruments (see p. 19). In the Concerto
and the Quintet, the melodic and formal structures of the movements seem to indicate that some passages were subjected to octave
transpositions or other alterations. These pieces were amended in
print, because Stadler's instrument was not well-known and they
could otherwise not have been played and therefore would have
sold badly. Among the passages which may have been altered are:

Concerto, third movement, bars 169 ff.

Most probably the quavers were originally all in the lowest register
and then were here, at the second and third appearance of the
figure, transposed to the octave above. The following passage,

Concerto, third movement, bars 311 ff.

extraordinarily difficult to execute and really the only one in the
Concerto unsuitable for the clarinet, today is played an octave
lower by some virtuosi (replacing *c* by *g*) and was probably also an
octave lower in the original. Finally, in the following passage

of the Quintet in the second trio of the minuet the first figure
would have matched to the other arpeggios thus:

In 1951 Dr Milan Kostohryz, professor of the clarinet at the Prague Conservatory, persuaded the maker Rudolf Trejbal to build a new lower section for his A clarinet, which, like a basset horn, had four keys for low e♭ down to *c*. In the same year in Prague, a pupil of Kostohryz, Josef Janous, played the probably original version of the Concerto for the first time; and in 1956 Kratochvil himself (he teaches the history and literature of wind instruments at the Academy of Fine Arts in Prague) played a reconstruction of the Quintet. It should perhaps be mentioned in passing that the Quintet contains considerably fewer passages which appear to have been altered.

Until recently, there was no contemporary evidence for these amendations, but this has now been provided by Ernst Hess in a lecture given in 28 August 1967 at a conference of the Central Institute for Mozart Research in Salzburg, shortly to be printed in the *Mozart Year Book*.[1] Hess referred to a review of the printed score of the Concerto in the *Leipziger Allgemeine Musikalische Zeitung* of March 1802, which contained the following passage: 'Finally, the critic feels obliged to say that Mozart wrote this Concerto for a clarinet encompassing low C. Thus, the following passages in the principal voice have all to be transposed from the lower octave' [here follow six examples] ... 'and similarly very many passages have been transposed or altered' [here follow further examples] ... 'However, since clarinets encompassing low C must at present be counted among the rarer instruments, thanks are due to the editors for these transpositions and alterations, although they have not improved the Concerto. Perhaps it would have been just as well to have published it in the original version and to have inserted these transpositions and alterations in smaller notes.'

At any rate, we know now that the Concerto was certainly written for the basset clarinet, and of the passages which the critic

[1] I should like to take this opportunity of thanking Professor Gerhard Kroll for sending me a copy of the lecture.

cited with music examples, we have the original versions. Unfortunately he did not illustrate every alteration, so that for the rest of the score we still depend on conjecture (see Kratochvil). So far as the first movement is concerned, the original draft of the first movement for basset horn in G provides further possibilities of reconstructing the original score (see Hess). We know, for instance, from the review, that the passage

Concerto, second movement, bars 49, 50

was originally scored thus:

In the Concerto[1] and the Quintet Mozart wrote beautifully for the clarinet, whose technical potentialities, considering the stage of its development at that time, he used to the full without, in the Quintet, allowing the clarinettist to dominate as a soloist. It seems almost incredible today that Stadler mastered these works on his primitive instrument, although the players of his time had much more practice in cross-fingering, which is only used in a few cases today. Mozart used the high register of the clarinet very sparingly but was all the more partial to the low tones of the instrument. He was most skilful in the juxtaposition of the different tone colours, as, for instance, in the following passage:

Concerto, first movement, bars 206 ff.

[1] Mozart's pupil, F. X. Süssmayer, also composed a Clarinet Concerto. In a letter to his wife (8 October 1791), Mozart wrote: 'Tell Süssmayer to get on with his writing for Stadler, for he has asked me particularly about it.' Draft scores for a Concerto for the A clarinet (in D major), dated 1792, by Süssmayer are in the British Museum.

18 Bass clarinet by Nicolo Papalini (Brussels Collection)

19 Contrabass clarinet (all metal) by Wilhelm Heckel, Biebrich. Total length of tube 9 feet: height about 4 feet

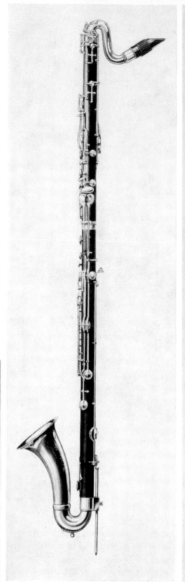

20 (left) Bass clarinet by J. Albert, Brussels

21 (above left) Bass clarinet, modern construction, to low *d*, by Arthur Uebel, Markneukirchen

22 Contrabass clarinet by G. H. Hüller, Schöneck

Mozart's use of the aptitude of the clarinet for the cantilena is particularly effective. The simple beauty of his tuneful adagio movements is imperishable.

Mozart left unfinished the scores for some clarinet quintets: an Allegro in B♭ (K.516c, appendix 91) completed to the end of the exposition; a few bars of a Rondo in E♭; a fragment of an Allegro in F belonging to a quintet for clarinet in C, basset horn in F, violin, viola, and cello; and finally a fragment of a Rondo in A for basset clarinet (K.581a, appendix 88). The notation in the latter piece is somewhat confusing in that it constantly changes from treble to bass and various C clefs. R. Tenschert who first drew attention to the fragment, interpreted this, perhaps rightly, as a practical joke at Stadler's expense. The four fragments, together with the Clarinet and Horn Quintets, are to be found in the volume *Quintette mit Bläsern* of the New Mozart Edition, edited by Ernst Fritz Schmid (published by Bärenreiter, 1958. See also its preface). In regard to notation, it should be said that Mozart did put some passages for the basset clarinet and the basset horn in bass clef. Like French horns, they then sound higher than the written notes, i.e. written *c′* in treble clef and written *c* in bass clef sound the same, i.e. on a basset horn in F, *f*.

Mention should be made of the enchanting little Duets for two basset horns (K.487), which have been variously arranged for other instruments but are at their best in the original, especially as few instruments have the required compass (three octaves and one fifth). The Duets make somewhat heavy demands on the first player (the part goes to *g‴* several times). Mozart used basset horns also in some Nocturnes and Canzonets for two soprano voices and bass, accompanied by three clarinets or basset horns (again in G!); in a little Cantonic Adagio for two basset horns and bassoon (K.410), the Masonic Funeral Music, the great B♭ Serenade for Wind Instruments (K.361), the *Magic Flute*, the *Requiem*, in an aria for *Figaro*, composed subsequently, and in *Die Entführung*.

The Adagio for two clarinets and three basset horns (K.411) is a magnificent piece (printed in the early edition of *Mozart's Complete Works*, series X, which also contains the Canonic Adagio and the Duets in series XXIV). There is an Allegro Assai in B♭ major, unfortunately only a fragment, for the same instruments, and an unfinished Adagio in F major for one clarinet and three basset horns.

Like the Quintet and the Concerto, the great solo parts in *Titus* were intended for Stadler, who journeyed to Prague for the first night of the opera and with great success played the clarinet solo in Sextus' aria 'Parto, ma tu ben mio', as well as the brilliant basset horn part in Vitellia's rondo. Some members of the audience and his colleagues in the orchestra ('Oh, miracle of Bohemia', he wrote) exclaimed 'Bravo!'. The clarinet solo descends down to *c* since Mozart wrote for Stadler's 'bass clarinet'.

While in his opera scores Mozart assigned to the clarinet a privileged position and often used it in serenades, he rarely employed it in symphonies. As a leading wind instrument, we find the clarinet for the first time in the Eb major Symphony (K.543) of 1788, in which there are no oboes, while in the G minor Symphony (K.550), composed at the same time, the more austere tone of the oboe prevails.[1]

In the Elector of Cologne's private orchestra at Bonn the clarinet was definitely in use by 1784, so that already in his boyhood Beethoven had opportunities of studying the qualities of the clarinet, especially as the wind instruments were there particularly well represented. A renowned author, Chaplain Junker, wrote the following passage in Bossler's *Musikalische Realzeitung* about the music played daily at meal-times (two oboes, two clarinets, two bassoons and two horns): 'These eight players may rightly be called masters of their art. One but rarely finds music of this kind played so harmoniously and with such a high degree of purity and perfection of tone.'

Two works by Beethoven, published posthumously and probably written specifically for these meal-time concerts, were an Octet Opus 103 and a Rondino (unnumbered), presumably composed in 1792. Although in both the oboe mostly takes the leading part, the clarinet also is made to carry the melody, and occasionally its

---

[1] Later Mozart divided the oboe parts between oboe and clarinet; see also New Mozart Edition, vol.9, *Symphonies*, edited by H. C. R. Landon, preface, p. x, and critical appraisal.

players have to execute some difficult figures. The three Duets for clarinet and bassoon (published in 1815) were probably written at the same time. Their melodies still show some typically 'Mannheim' features. Technically they are not too easy and give good evidence of the skill of the Bonn clarinettists.

About 1796–97 in Vienna, Beethoven composed his marvellous Quintet for wind instruments, Opus 16, in which, unlike Mozart, he gives the leading part to the clarinet. At approximately the same time, he wrote the Sextet Opus 71, for two clarinets, two horns and two bassoons. In 1798 there followed the Trio Opus 11 for clarinet, cello and piano, which is said to have been written for a clarinettist at whose request Beethoven chose as the theme for the variations a popular tune from Weigl's favourite opera *L'Amor marinaro* (*Der Korsar*, 1797). If in this work the clarinet part is not invariably in harmony with the character of the instrument, in his Septet[1] Opus 20, composed in 1800, Beethoven assigned an all the more rewarding task to the clarinettist.

Regrettably, Beethoven's friendship with the outstanding Vienna clarinettist, Joseph Friedlowsky,[2] did not inspire him to further compositions with solo clarinet. We know only that Beethoven frequently asked Friedlowsky for information about the mechanism of the clarinet and its tonal and technical characteristics, so that he knew the instrument more intimately and was able to compose for it far more daringly than for other wind instruments. The Trio of the Minuet in the Eighth Symphony provides a typical example:

Beethoven also wrote magnificently for the clarinet as a cantabile instrument and one of the most beautiful tunes ever composed for it is contained in the Adagio of the Septet.

---

[1] Two years later, Beethoven arranged the Septet as a Trio for clarinet, cello and piano and published it as Opus 38.

[2] The clarinet part of Spohr's Octet Opus 32 (1814) was written for Friedlowsky.

The virtuoso era

The popularity of wind instrument virtuosi reached its height in the concluding decade of the eighteenth and the first two decades of the nineteenth century. According to reports from Vienna, there were in that city many more wind-instrument soloists than solo violinists or even pianists. In addition to the many concerts given by visiting soloists, every soloist in the theatre orchestra had his own annual concert and also was frequently asked to play at the so-called 'academies'. However, in the third decade of the nineteenth century the popularity of wind instrument solos gradually decreased so that by the middle of the century violinists, cellists and pianists had largely replaced the wind soloists, and although the latter still gave many concerts, they did so to half-empty halls. In 1866 the critic Eduard Hanslick advised the clarinet-tist Romeo Orsi, who had given a concert in Vienna, to 'join an orchestra. That is the place where we like to see the players of clarinet, oboe and bassoon; the times are passed when crowds of these artists came from everywhere to perform on their boring little pipes.'[1] But only a few years later Hanslick was obliged to eat at least some of his words. 'In principle, the end of the flood of flute, oboe, bassoon and clarinet concerts was most welcome, because these instruments need and supply some accompaniment and as such belong to the orchestra, especially as they have no classical literature of their own. But the terrible spread of the piano, an independent but already most intrusive instrument, makes us more kindly disposed towards the dethroned wind players, and we would not be adverse to hearing, for example, a virtuoso performance of one of the beautiful Clarinet Concertos by C. M. Weber.'

Innumerable clarinettists were being trained towards the end of the eighteenth century. At the founding of the Paris Conservatoire (1795) no less than 12 clarinet teachers were appointed who,

[1] As early as 1792–93, Kunzen-Reichardt's *Musikalisches Wochenblatt* attacked the solo wind instruments. 'Why cannot we bear wind instruments?' asked one article and the following supplied the answer: 'About the Shorter Duration of Our Pleasure in the Playing of Wind Instruments'. The article accused soloists and composers of lack of skill.

altogether, had 104 pupils.[1] Most of the musicians trained here and at other places found work with military bands, some of which employed up to twenty clarinettists. Among the wind instrumentalists in these bands, as in theatre and concert orchestras, there were many outstanding performers who often took several months' or even years' leave, and periodically renounced firm employment altogether, in order to tour Europe and give successful concerts everywhere. The following list supplies the names of some of the best-known clarinet virtuosi:

Abrahame	?–1805	Kleine, J. W.	1815–?
Backofen, J. G. H.	1768–1839	Klosé, K. E.	1808–1880
Baermann, H. J.	1784–1847	Kotte, J. G.	1797–1857
Baermann, C.	1811–1885	Krähmer, Caroline,	
Beer, J.	1744–1811	née Schleicher	1794–?
Beerhalter, A.	1800–1852	Lazarus, H.	1815–1895
Bender, J.	1798–1844	Lefèvre, J. X.	1763–1829
Bender, V.	1801–1873	Meissner, P.	1748–1816
Berr, F.	1794–1838	Mühlfeld, R.	1856–1907
Blaes, A. J.	1814–1892	Müller, F.	1786–1871
Blasius, F.	1758–1829	Müller, Ivan	1786–1854
Blatt, F. T.	1793–?	Pisarowitz, J.	?–1881
Bliesener, F. A.	1780–1841	Poncelet, G.	1845–1903
Cavallini, E.	1807–1874	Reinhardt, G.	1789–?
Canongia, A. J.	1784–1842	Roth, G.	1769–1817
Christiani, P. X.	1787–1867	Sebastiani, F.	1808–1860
Crusell, B. H.	1775–1838	Seeman	1793–?
Dacosta, I. F.	1778–1866	Sobeck, J.	1831–1914
David, A.	c. 1730–1796	Springer, V.	c. 1760–?
Duvernoy, C.	1766–1845	Stadler, A.	1753–1812
Farnik, W.	1770–1838	Stadler, J.	1756–1804
Faubel, J.	1801–?	Stark, R.	1847–1922
Friedlowsky, A.	1804–1875	Tausch, Franz	1762–1817
Friedlowsky, J.	1777–1859	Tausch, Joseph	1763–?
Fuchs, G. F.	1752–1821	Tausch, F. W.	c. 1790–1845
Gambaro, G. B.	1785–1828	Vanderhagen, A.	1753–1822
Göpfert, C. A.	1768–1818	Willman, T. L.	c. 1774–1840
Hermstedt, J. S.	1778–1846	Yost, Michel	1754–1786

[1] There were only eight flautists with 32 pupils, and six oboists with 24.

This enormous number of clarinet soloists naturally consumed a great deal of solo music and as the public continued to ask for new, hitherto unknown works, every virtuoso sought to perform music not available to his competitors. Many soloists commissioned popular composers to write concertos and concert pieces for considerable fees and on condition that they were guaranteed the sole performing rights for a certain period. In addition, many virtuosi themselves composed music for their instruments so as to be certain to present their public with new works.

Franz Tausch may be regarded as the founder of a long line of clarinet virtuosi. Not counting his predecessor, G. F. Fuchs, he was the first representative of the player-composer type of artist of the clarinet. He probably wrote a great number of works, of which four concertos (among them two double concertos for two clarinets), and 'Andante and Polonaise' and several duets for two clarinets and clarinet and bassoon, are extant. In his concertos Tausch laid great stress on virtuosity (see p. 57).

Among the composing clarinet virtuosi, J. Beer, F. Blasius, J. X. Lefèvre, J. G. H. Backofen, the Finn B. H. Crusell, Ivan Müller, Friedrich Müller (no relation of the last), C. Göpfert, F. Berr, Heinrich and Carl Baermann, should be mentioned as authors of concertos. Among the popular composers and those writing music for special occasions, were Bendler, Bochsa, F. Cramer, F. S. Destouches, M. Eberwein, Gebauer, Gohrlich, Grua, Habermehl, Heinze, Hostié, Kreibe, Konradin Kreutzer, F. Krommer, P. von Lindpaintner, L. Maurer, C. H. Meyer, Mourin, H. Panofka, Pfeilstiker, Poessinger, K. G. Reissiger, J. Rietz, P. J. Riotte, F. A. Rosetti (or Rössler), J. Schenk, L. Schindelmeisser (concerto for four clarinets), J. Schnabel, A. Schneider, Stumpf, Vandenbroeck, Vogel, C. M. Westerhoff, Wilms, Wratni.

Besides concertos and concert pieces, variations and fantasias on themes from popular operas or other tunes were fashionable. To name but a few of these works—some of them written in later years—which are still known and, because of their technical difficulties, often used for study purposes: C. Baermann, *Souvenirs de Bellini*: L. Bassi, Fantasia on *Rigoletto*: F. David, Introduction and Variations on Schubert's *Sehnsuchtswalzer*: Franke, Variations and

Rondo on a theme from *Die Stumme von Portici*: Unger, *Faust* Fantasia: J. G. Georg, Fantasia on *Der Freischütz*[1]: T. Müngersdorf, Fantasia on the best Arias from Mozart's operas: J. Sobeck, Fantasia on Motifs from *Jessonda*: A. Schreiner, Fantasia on *Oberon*: A. Wallnöfer, Meditation on the Adagio in Beethoven's Moonlight Sonata (!). Duets for two clarinets, also arrangements of popular melodies, were always in demand, especially towards the end of the eighteenth and the beginning of the nineteenth century. But all these compositions still did not suffice to satisfy the itinerant clarinettists, let alone the amateurs. The gaps were filled by various arrangements; for example, the most popular arias from operas and oratorios were arranged for clarinet and piano[2] and, in some instances, whole overtures.

It is impossible at the present day to give an adequate description of the innumerable compositions and arrangements dating from that period. Most of them are run-of-the-mill pieces without any merit, designed to afford more than ample opportunities to the players of showing their skill in the execution of the most boring and monotonous scales and chord figures. The concertos by Ivan Müller, some compositions by Carl Baermann, and an effective concertino by Reissiger which is rather better than the name 'Study Concerto' implies, are still in demand for practice purposes. A Concerto by Riotte and one (F minor) by Crusell, and Rossini's Introduction, Theme and Variations have recently been republished (all three edited by J. Michaels); Franz Krommer wrote some charming concertos (Concerto in E♭, Opus 36: concerto for two clarinets, republished in Prague, edited by J. Kratochvil, available from Bärenreiter). (The real name of the Bohemian Krommer was František Kramář, and he is occasionally somewhat misleadingly referred to as Kramar-Krommer.)

The compositions by C. M. von Weber and Louis Spohr, on the other hand, are of lasting value. According to Schletterer (see introduction), Spohr wrote a concert piece (*Konzertstück*) for a Brunswick clarinettist as early as 1804 or 1805, though this appears

---

[1] Inexplicably republished by Schroeder, Berlin, as Op. 6 by F. Kroepsch.

[2] E.g. the aria of the page from *Les Huguenots*, the mercy aria from *Robert the Devil*, the picture aria from *The Magic Flute*, the cavatine from *The Barber of Seville*, the aria from Rossini's *Stabat Mater*, etc.

to have been lost. Some years later, Spohr received more effective inspiration from the brilliant Sondershausen clarinettist J. S. Hermstedt. In his autobiography he gives an account of his first meeting with the virtuoso.

> In one of these concerts [a subscription concert in Gotha], Herr Hermstedt, director of music to the Duke of Sondershausen, performed on the clarinet and caused a sensation by his virtuosity, already at that time highly developed. He had come to Gotha to ask me for a clarinet concerto, for which his Duke was willing to pay a considerable sum on condition that Hermstedt should become the owner of the manuscript. I was very willing to fall in with the suggestion, especially as Hermstedt's immense skill, as well as his beautiful tone and pure intonation, gave me the opportunity of giving full rein to my imagination. After Hermstedt had helped me to familiarise myself with the technique of the instrument, my work proceeded rapidly and was completed inside a few weeks. That was the origin of the C minor Concerto which Kühnel engraved some years later as Opus 26 and with which Hermstedt was so successful on his tours that it is not too much to say that he owes much of his reputation to it. I myself handed it to him on a visit to Sondershausen at the end of January (1809) and gave him some hints as to how it should be performed.

Spohr attached an interesting 'Reminder' to the printed version of the Concerto:

> I herewith present clarinettists with a Concerto, composed two years ago for my friend, musical director Hermstedt of Sondershausen. At that time my knowledge of the instrument was more or less confined to its compass, so that I took too little account of its weaknesses and wrote some passages which, at first glance, may seem impossible of execution. However, Herr Hermstedt, far from asking me to make changes, sought rather to perfect his instrument, and by constant application, soon attained such mastery that his clarinet produced no more jarring, muffled or uncertain notes. In subsequent compositions for him I was able, therefore, to give free rein to my pen and had no need to fear that anything might be impossible to him.[1] Herr Hermstedt and other good clarinettists suggested the following amendments without which the Concerto could not be properly performed: 1. A key for low E♭ and

[1] On the other hand, Schletterer (introduction) states: 'Henceforth Spohr wrote all his clarinet works for his friend Hermstedt and never tired of altering and amending them until they seemed practicable and rewarding to the player, showed his technique in the most favourable light and brought out the harmonious sound of the instrument to full advantage.'

the trills D–E♭ and A–B♭, for the first[1] finger of the right hand (also called B♭ key). 2. A key for the middle F and the trills E–F and B–C, for the third[2] finger of the left hand. 3. A key for the trills A–B and B♭–C for the first finger of the right hand. 4. A key for middle A♭ for the first finger of the left hand (next to the A key). 5. A key for the low B♭ and the trills low A–B♭ and middle E–F, for the third finger of the right hand. 6. Two adjoining holes for the third finger of the left hand, for a true low C♯ or, preferably, for the same purpose a key for the little finger of the left hand. 7. A hole on the lower side of the clarinet to be covered by the thumb of the right hand, for low B. 8. Both the long keys curved in such a way as to enable the player to sound the medium B and C♯ in quick succession. For the passages which go beyond the normal compass of the instrument, altered versions for those that cannot reach the high c″″, are given in small notes in the solo part. May this Concerto induce other composers for the clarinet (surely the most perfect of wind instruments if played in the way Herr Hermstedt does) to avoid the monotony of most existing clarinet compositions, which largely consist of the repetition of technically simple and terribly trite soloistic passages, and to look for wider fields for an instrument so rich in compass and expression.

The First Concerto was followed in 1810 by a second in E♭ major, in 1821 by a third in F minor and in 1829 by a fourth (for A clarinet) in E minor. In the intervals Spohr wrote some smaller pieces: Variations Opus 80 on themes from P. von Winter's *Opferfest* (1811), a Fantasia with variations on a theme by Danzi Opus 81 (1814) and Variations from *Alruna*.

These works are not in every respect suitable for the clarinet, i.e. they are not minutely adapted to the technical and tonal capa-bilities of the instrument as are Weber's compositions. On the contrary, some characteristics point very clearly to Spohr's intimate relations with the violin, for example the little trills which are so typical of his violin pieces:

Third Concerto, second movement

---

[1] The thumb is not counted here, so that the index finger, as in playing the violin, is reckoned the first finger.
[2] According to Spohr's numbering, should be 'second'.

Also certain chord figures:

First Concerto, first movement

and the frequent flourishes in the slow movements.

Spohr showed surprising boldness in making use of the high register of the clarinet in rapid figuration. An example is to be found in the third movement of the Third Concerto:

Regrettably, the Octet Opus 32 (clarinet, two horns, strings) is rarely performed today. In 1837 Spohr wrote, at the request of the Duchess of Sondershausen, the enchanting *Sechs deutsche Lieder* Opus 103, for voice, clarinet and piano, which offer rewarding opportunities to the player as a virtuoso and musician.

Spohr was by no means the first composer to create songs with solo clarinet accompaniment. Franz Schubert first wrote an Offertory *Totus in corde langueo* Opus 46, for soprano, solo clarinet, orchestra and organ, and in 1828 the much sung *Der Hirt auf dem Felsen* ('The Shepherd on the Rock') Opus 129, for soprano, clarinet and piano,[1] dedicated to Anna Milder-Hauptmann,[2] which contains an extremely effective clarinet part. Friedrich Silcher wrote *Serenade an Selma* for tenor, lute and clarinet; Meyerbeer composed an indifferent *Hirtenlied* for tenor, clarinet and piano, which he dedicated to Gustav Roger, the leading singer of his *Le Prophète*, and also a cantata *Thecelindens Liebschaften* for soprano, obbligato clarinet (for H. Baermann) and orchestra; and in 1847 Franz Lachner composed his *Lied* Opus 82 *Seit ich ihn gesehen*.

Almost at the same time as Spohr, Weber wrote his unforgettable

---

[1] Carl Reinicke has published an edition with orchestral accompaniment.
[2] A famous singer (1785–1838) and the first Leonore in Beethoven's *Fidelio*.

works for the clarinet. His inspiration was the eminent Munich clarinet virtuoso Heinrich Baermann, whom he first met in Darmstadt in 1811, and whose integrity and sincere devotion to his art won Weber's affection for life. In the words of Max M. von Weber, 'although they rarely met in later life, their cordial friendship remained unimpaired' (*C. M. von Weber*, 1864–6).

While in Darmstadt, Weber composed for Baermann a Duet *Se il mio ben* for two contralto voices, solo clarinet, horn, and string quintet, and a little later in Munich he wrote and dedicated to his friend, the Concertino Opus 26, whose first performance was enthusiastically received. 'Since I composed the Concertino for Baermann, the whole orchestra has gone mad and demands concertos from me. They are pestering the King and the management', Weber wrote to his friend Gottfried Weber. Soon he was commissioned to write among other works two clarinet concertos. The first in F minor Opus 73 was completed in May 1811, the second in E♭ major Opus 74 in July of the same year. In December, while on a concert tour with Baermann in Prague, he wrote the Variations Opus 33 on a theme from *Sylvana*, and this work had its first performance on the day it was completed.[1]

Already in September 1811, Weber began the Clarinet Quintet Opus 34 which was not finished until 1815, although he gave the first three movements to Baermann as a birthday present in 1813.[2] Weber's last composition for the clarinet, and the only one not dedicated to Baermann,[3] was the magnificent *Grand Duo Concertant* Opus 48, which he completed in November 1816.

Together with the works of Mozart, Weber's clarinet music is the most valued possession of the clarinettist. Brilliantly exploiting the technical and musical potentialities of the instrument, it presents

[1] According to Carl Baermann, the solo part of the adagio variations was composed by his father but the much simpler part in that edition printed at the top was probably by Weber, while the lower is much more in keeping with H. Baermann's style.

[2] Despite the chamber-music character of the work, Bernhard Kutsch later arranged it as a clarinet concerto and had it published by Robert Lienau.

[3] The work may have been intended for Hermstedt who, in 1812, offered Weber 10 louis d'or for a concerto. The composer promised to consider the suggestion. In 1815 Weber noted in his diary: 'Worked . . . on clarinet concerto for Hermstedt.' As Weber left no work of this nature, it may be assumed that the work referred to was used in the 'Duo' Weber played on 10 and 17 February in Prague with Hermstedt.

the player with a rewarding task, since it is perfectly adjusted
to the character of the clarinet and thus affords him the opportunity
of showing himself at his best. Take, for instance, the most effective
and dramatic opening of the E♭ major Concerto, and in the Concertino the wonderful use of the dark, low register whose eerie,
mournful sounds Weber so readily used in the opera orchestra:

and, especially in the third movement of the Duo, the transition
to the triumphant reprise.

Weber was most economical in the use of the high notes of the
instrument and rarely took it higher than *f'''*. The highest notes are
employed very cautiously in the first movement of the E♭ major
Concerto:

In 1870 Carl Baermann re-edited Weber's clarinet music and had
it published by the contemporary firm of Schlesinger. Unfortunately the editor proceeded somewhat arbitrarily. He may have
followed tradition but the work he produced is hardly in keeping
with the composer's intentions.[1]

The second half of the last and the first years of the present
century have produced little in the way of concert pieces for the

[1] The Berlin chamber-music soloist Leonhard Kohl discovered in 1943 a hitherto
unknown composition by C. M. von Weber. The copy bears the title 'Concerto for
clarinet and string quartet' but in fact the work consists of variations of a virtuoso
character, based entirely on the technical capabilities of the clarinet. It may be
assumed that this is the composition referred to by M. M. von Weber when he says:
'On 15 July 1885, in Munich a piece of music was completed for friend Baermann's
name day but it has disappeared.' It has since been published under the title 'Introduction, Theme and Variations' in Berlin (Afas; also in clarinet and piano arrangement).

clarinet and few of these can make any claim to excellence. The most interesting and valuable work of the period is Max Bruch's Double Concerto for clarinet, viola and orchestra. For a long time it was believed lost but it was finally discovered in private owner-ship in Hamburg and subsequently published. The composition originated in 1911 in Bad Wildungen and had an extremely success-ful first performance in 1940 with Alfred Burkner, Reinhard Wolf and the Berlin Philharmonic Orchestra.[1]

Concertos, fantasias, variations and similar works were also composed among others by H. Franke, K. Friedemann, C. Gurlitt, M. Heidrich, J. F. Hummel,[2] L. Kempter, J. G. H. Mann, F. Manns, J. Meurer, L. Milde, G. Pittrich (Concerto in E♭ major, which received a prize), T. H. H. Verhey, and by the clarinettists E. Caval-lini, E. Gabler, G. Haseneier, H. E. Klosé, J. Sobeck and R. Stark. For study purposes, some of these works are still popular, e.g. the concertos by Mann, Gabler and Stark; and the Fantasia by Kempter and the concert piece by Milde. In France, several compositions by Klosé, revised by P. Jeanjean, are very popular indeed. One or other of the works referred to may occasionally be heard on the radio but unfortunately not very often, although some of them still retain their value.

The clarinet in chamber music

When in the second third of the past century, public interest in wind instrument virtuosi decreased, most wind instruments lost their importance as solo instruments with the exception of the clarinet, which maintained its position, not so much as solo instru-ment but as an ideal chamber music instrument—as it had long been known—and by virtue of the discovery made in that period that its tone harmonised beautifully with that of the piano.

Franz Danzi's Sonata, and the Archduke Rudolf's unpublished

[1] Rimsky-Korssakov also wrote a Clarinet Concerto which, however, cannot be com-pared with his big orchestral works.
[2] His second Concerto in F minor was again made generally available when it was published by the Salzburg Hummel-Gemeinde.

Variations on a Cavatina by Rossini, of which the autograph, with corrections by Beethoven, is preserved by the Vienna Society of the Friends of Music, were among the first works for clarinet and piano. Among them are also Weber's *Grand Duo Concertant* and Heinrich Baermann's Sonata Opus 33 (1827 ?), both written in the virtuoso tradition, and a Sonata by Beethoven's pupil Ferdinand Ries, as well as a Duet by Norbert Burgmüller who died at an early age. In the 1840s Carl Baermann published some chamber music for clarinet and piano, and in 1849, Robert Schumann his enchanting *Fantasiestücke* Opus 73.[1]

Two of Lefèvre's Sonatas (D minor and B♭ major) are in print. Vanhal's Sonata has already been mentioned. The E♭ major Sonata by Mendelssohn, a work of his youth, as yet shows little character, but the two Concert Pieces in D minor and F minor for clarinet and basset horn with piano accompaniment (written for Heinrich and Carl Baermann) are most effective, particularly the second. Unfortunately, these pieces are published only in arrangements. (The original version is in the early edition of Mendelssohn's Complete Works.) Jost Michaels, the professor for clarinet at the Detmold Muscial Academy, arranged them for two clarinets, and has done an invaluable service by publishing other forgotten clarinet works. There is also an arrangement for clarinet and bassoon.

The concertante duets by F. R. Gebauer, Opus 2 for two clarinets and Opus 8 for clarinet and bassoon are suitable for study purposes (Gebauer also wrote six brilliant concertante trios for clarinet, horn and bassoon). There are numerous similar duets; those by Cavallini, B. Crusell, Gebauer, Devienne, and by Stadler (together with duets by Crusell), have been recently republished.

In the second half of the century, so many works were written for clarinet and piano that it is impossible to give even an approximately exhaustive list. To mention only a few: in 1850 Karl Loewe wrote *Schottische Bilder* for his son-in-law, an amateur clarinettist. These pieces have descriptive titles and are of little significance. In 1864 Nils W. Gade published his *Fantasiestücke* Opus 43, dedicated to the Copenhagen clarinettist Mozart Petersen.

---

[1] Schumann's Romances Opus 94 were intended for the oboe but are very effective on the clarinet.

Karl Reinecke also wrote for the clarinet and, in 1865, published the *Fantasiestücke* Opus 22, followed in 1901 by *Introduzione ed Allegro appassionato* Opus 256, dedicated to Mühlfeld. August Winding's *Fantasiestücke* Opus 19, printed in 1872, were very well received and highly praised by Hans von Bülow. A Sonata Opus 67 by Théodore Gouvy, though not outstanding in invention and execution, is remarkable as the first indication of Gouvy's preference for wind instruments. The work, composed in 1875 and published seven years later, was followed in 1888 by a refreshingly tuneful Sonata Opus 38 by Felix Draesecke, a composer who should not have been allowed to fall into oblivion, and in 1893 by the attractive Sonata Opus 105a, by Joseph Rheinberger. Two years later J. Brahms wrote his unforgettable Sonatas Opus 120.

Trios for the clarinet were a good deal rarer. Mozart's 'Kegelstatt Trio' was probably one of the first important works of this type. It was followed by Beethoven's two trios and a little later by a trio for clarinet, cello and piano by Ferdinand Ries. In 1826–27, Mikhai Glinka composed his *Trio pathétique* for clarinet, bassoon and piano, and Konradin Kreutzer's Trio Opus 43, with the same instrumentation, was probably written at about the same time or not much later. For some years after that no trio compositions worth mentioning were written until 1835, when in search of new fields of expression, Robert Schumann composed his *Märchenerzählungen* Opus 132 for clarinet, viola and piano, which is one of the very best clarinet works and marks a magnificent climax in the master's total output.

Quintets for clarinet with string quartet are rarer even than clarinet trios. Mozart's work of this kind for a long time remained unique in its perfection. Other clarinet quintets with solo, almost concerto-like clarinet parts were written by Weber, Spohr, Heinrich and Carl Baermann, and the famous Prague clarinettist Franz Thaddäus Blatt. Anton Reicha, Andreas Romberg, the son of an outstanding clarinettist, and the violin virtuoso Thomas Täglichsbeck wrote quintets for the same instrumentation, which, however, were very little known or soon forgotten.

Reicha's Quintet has recently been reprinted, as also a charming Quartet by Hummel, the second movement of which, entitled

'La Seccatura', appears at first glance to contain rhythmical difficulties (the clarinet part is in 2/4, the violin in 12/8. the viola in 3/4
and the cello in 6/8 time). Crusell wrote a Quartet with the same
instrumentation but Brahms was the first composer to create a work
which may be regarded as equal to Mozart's.[1]

Brahm's chamber music represents a climax in the history of
clarinet music, subsequently reached also by Max Reger but never
surpassed. The two Sonatas, the Trio and the Quintet, all created
in the last, most mature working period of the master, and of
uniform excellence, contain his most profound thought and are
wonderfully at one with the spirit and character of the clarinet.
Here the instrument is put through the whole range of its expressive
possibilities, without there being any places to overtax technical
skill. An occasional bar offers certain difficulties, e.g. the demi-
semiquaver runs in the Presto of the Quintet, the sextuplet runs
in the last movement of the Trio, and the following passage in the
Adagio of the Quintet.

Brahms dedicated all four of his clarinet works to his friend, the
clarinettist Richard Mühlfeld of Meiningen, whose playing often
gave him great pleasure. He composed the Trio and the Quintet
at Ischl in the summer of 1891, having received detailed instructions
by Mühlfeld as to the technical and tonal qualities of the clarinet.
On 25 July Brahms announced both compositions in a jocular letter
to the Baroness Heldburg of Meiningen. Several days previously he
had informed his friend Mandyczewski in Vienna that the Trio 'was
the twin of an even greater folly' which he was now trying to
'coax out'. At the end of November of the same year, Brahms,
Mühlfeld and the Joachim Quartet tried out both works in Meinin-

---

[1] According to Hans-Georg Bach, the Adagio for clarinet and string quintet contained
in the complete works of Wagner, vol. xx, is by H. J. Baermann.

23 Heckelphone clarinet, clarinet in
A♮ (length, 14½ inches), clarinet in E♭,
clarinet in C. All four instruments
by Wilhelm Heckel, Biebrich

24 Soprano saxophone by Deprins,
Antwerp (about 1900)

25 Bass saxophone by A. Rampone,
Milan (total length four times that of
soprano saxophone). Both saxophones
in the collection of the Staatliches
Institut für Musikforschung, Berlin

26 Anton Stadler (1753–1812)

27 Stadler's 'bass clarinet' (clarine[
in A with four basset keys, down t[
written *c*). Modern replica by Rud[
Trejbal of Prague. Owned by Dr V[
Rey of Münster. For comparison (l[
a normal A-clarinet (Oehler system[

gen, and the first public performance took place on 12 December in Berlin at one of Joachim's 'quartet soirées'.[1] Thanks largely to the brilliant clarinettist, both Trio and Quintet met with great success and the audience demanded an encore of the Adagio in the Quintet.

Three years later, in July 1894, Brahms wrote the two Clarinet Sonatas, in F minor and E♭ major, works of the ultimate and highest mastery. In the Trio and the Quintet Brahms had used the A clarinet to express dark passions and resignation; he wrote the lively Sonatas for the brighter B♭ instrument. Mühlfeld played in the first performances in Vienna on 7, 8 and 11 January 1895. In a relatively short time, Brahms' clarinet works became known all over the world through Mühlfeld's concert tours, but in spite of their enormous success, the compositions failed to inspire other composers, although at the request of Brahms the Vienna Tonkünstlerverein (Musicians' Association) organised a prize competition for 'the furtherance of wind-instrument music'. The prize, which Brahms had increased out of his own pocket, went to Nawratil's pupil Walther Rabl, whose Quartet for clarinet, violin, cello and piano was published in 1897 at the instigation of Brahms.

Among other noteworthy works of the subsequent years are the Sonata Opus 5 by Gustav Jenner (1900) and the clarinet Quintets Opus 19, by Stephan Krehl (1902), and Opus 13 by Henri Marteau (1909). Trios for clarinet, cello and piano were composed amongst others, by Vincent d'Indy (Op.29), Alexander Zemlinsky (Op.3, 1897), Wilhelm Berger (Op.94, 1905, dedicated to Mühlfeld), and Johan Amberg (Op.11, 1912). The latter also wrote a Trio for clarinet, viola and piano (Op.12, 1911), as did Karl Reinecke (Op.264, 1903) and Max Bruch (Eight Pieces, Op.38, 1910). Maximilian Heidrich (Op.25, 1894), Alexander Friedrich, Landgrave of Hesse (Op.3, 1897), and Karl Reinecke (Op.274, 1906) scored for clarinet, horn and piano. Rarely used instrumentations were chosen by Waldemar von Bausznern for his Serenade in E♭ major for violin, clarinet and piano (1905), Maximilian Heidrich for his Trio Opus 33, for clarinet,

---

[1] Mühlfeld's playing at this concert inspired Adolf von Menzel to a sketch in Indian ink of a clarinettist in dinner jacket with leaves in his hair, like a muse, with the caption, 'Only Euterpe herself could have played a certain passage in a certain —— like that. A.M.' Menzel sent it to Brahms who had a photograph made for Mühlfeld of this 'most flatteringly unlike' portrait.

viola and cello (1911), and Paul Juon for his Divertimento Opus 34 for clarinet and two violas (1908). Hans Pfitzner composed a Sextet (Op.55) for clarinet, piano, violin, viola, cello and double bass. But none of these works stood the test of time, however meritorious and successful they may have been once. It was Max Reger who again created unforgettable works for the clarinet, reaching heights first attained by Brahms.

Reger's two Sonatas Opus 49 (Ab major and F# minor) were written in 1900, at a time when Reger was in Weiden living almost like a hermit and far removed from any music. But it happened that the director of the municipal orchestra, Johann Kürmeyer, was also a brilliant clarinettist and Reger heard a performance by him and Adalbert Lindner of Brahm's F minor Sonata. 'Lovely', said Reger, 'I also will write two of these things.' Within three weeks he had written the two Sonatas. His next clarinet work,[1] the great Sonata Opus 107 in Bb major, immediately followed the Symphonic Prologue, whose score was sent to the printers on 27 December 1908. The following day found Reger immersed in work on the Sonata, and on 20 February 1909 he joyfully announced its completion to his friend Max Straube. The first performance of both Sonatas Opus 49 took place on 18 April 1902, in Munich, by Karl Wagner and Max Reger, and Opus 107 was first performed at the second chamber music festival in Darmstadt, 7–9 June 1909, by Julius Winkler and again the composer.

A closer study of the three Sonatas by Reger reveals a certain similarity with the compositions by Brahms. The Sonatas Opus 49 were, indeed, composed while Reger felt the immediate impression of Brahms' Sonata, and Brahms thenceforth continued to be his model. A few days after starting work on the Bb major Sonata, Reger wrote in a letter, 'My new Sonata for clarinet and pianoforte is making good progress; it will be an uncommonly clear work; you can't allot overmuch "technique" to a wind player because there is always a danger of the chamber music style going by the board and the whole thing becoming a concertino, which would

[1] In 1902 Reger published as a music supplement to *Musikwoche* an 'Albumblatt' and a Tarantella of clarinet or violin with piano accompaniment, Both are charming little pieces, though not of the quality of Reger's other compositions. They have recently been reprinted.

be too bad. Brahms has set a pattern for what the style should be.'
The two Sonatas Opus 49 are among the most masterly works ever
written for the clarinet; every single movement is magnificent in
its line, its harmonies and its spiritual content—and yet the later
B♭ major Sonata represents a fresh climax compared with those
earlier works.

The Clarinet Quintet in A major Opus 146, the last finished
composition of the master, is the crowning achievement of Reger's
life work. The ideas and plans for it occupied his mind as early as
1912 but composition was repeatedly postponed in favour of other
works; in the end, the Quintet became his swan song. It was pre-
ceeded by *Der Einsiedler* and the *Requiem*, works created in the
sombre mood of one who felt death approaching and suffered
grievously from the horrors of the world war. In the Clarinet
Quintet Reger has overcome his sorrow. The whole work flows
serenely and lovably in harmonious contentment and ends with
variations bubbling over with ideas.

New literature

After the brilliant creations of Brahms and Reger, public interest
in the clarinet as a chamber music instrument seemed to become
strangely paralysed. But today, thanks to the efforts of outstanding
players and chamber music circles, the clarinet has regained its
rightful place in the concert hall, especially as the radio has for
many years made wide use of the solo player. Numerous works
with solo clarinet have been written in recent decades, and most of
them far exceed the level of the average work composed at the
turn of the century. Some may well gain a lasting place in the
repertoire of the clarinettist.[1]

Among the works for clarinet and orchestra to be mentioned
here are the Rhapsody by Claude Debussy (1910), the Concertino

[1] It should be noted that reference to or critique of a particular work in these pages
does not necessarily imply that it is of greater value than other compositions not mentioned. In principle, the author has dealt only with works available in print and with
manuscripts well known to him through his activities as a soloist.

by Ferruccio Busoni (1919), the Concerto by Robert Bückmann
(1939), and *Musik* by Erich Sehlbach (1942). Though the latter piece
is remarkable for its expressive tunefulness and noble melodies, the
other three represent a novel challenge to the player's technique.
Busoni and Debussy, in particular, make exceedingly great demands
on tone cultivation and production. For instance, how daring is the
as soft as possible pianissimo, *e'''* at the very beginning of Busoni's
Concertino, and how difficult the delicate tone colours throughout
Debussy's Rhapsody! In addition, Busoni, Debussy and Bückmann
often indulge in bold, complicated tonal combinations and occasionally difficult figures even in the highest range. It has rightly
been said that these works have advanced the skill of clarinettists
by a considerable amount. Gerhard Frommel, in his Concerto for
piano, solo clarinet and string orchestra (1935), sought new ways of
instrumental combination and concerto form. His unique work
also presents the player with several difficult technical problems.

Igor Stravinsky broke new ground when in 1919 he wrote 'Three
Pieces for the Solo Clarinet', an important work for unaccompanied
clarinet. These curious pieces, technically demanding and intended
specifically for the Boehm clarinet, were followed by the somewhat
difficult 'Stimmungen eines Fauns' by Ilse Fromm-Michaels, and
the musically and technically interesting Sonata Opus 110 by Siegfried Karg-Elert (1925) which shows much knowledge of the
instrument, and finally (1928) the Theme with Variations Opus 14
by Jørgen Bentzon, perhaps mainly intended for study purposes
and as such suitable and valuable. The best item in this group,
published in 1937, though composed six years earlier, is Hubert
Pfeiffer's 'Music for Unaccompanied A Clarinet', a most interesting
work of a highly personal character. Its underlying idea sprang
from the desire to create some polyphonic music for the clarinet
having two parts moving on two different levels. In other words,
two melody lines, each consisting of short thematic passages and
rests, are interwoven in such a way that the rests of one line coincide
with the notes of the other. In the final movement of the 'Music'
this apparent polyphony culminates in a veritable fugue.

Other composers to write for the unaccompanied clarinet are
H. Sutermeister (Capriccio, 1947), B. Kunc (Pastorale Fantasia Opus

59), L. de Lorenzo, Osborne (Rhapsody), and E. Wellesz (Suite Opus 74). The *Monologues* (1956) by Ernst Krenek are outstanding. However, performances of works for unaccompanied clarinet will probably always present a bit of a problem to the players as well as to the audience.

Foremost among works for clarinet and piano is Egon Kornauth's spirited and effective Sonata Opus 5 (composed 1912–13, published 1922) whose invention and theme-formation breathe the spirit of the new era, although the harmonies are still largely traditional.[1] Also noteworthy is E. Adaiewsky's *Greek Sonata* (1913) because the composer strove to combine 'material first consolidated by the Greeks in a tonal system—still extant in Slav church and folk music —with the tonal system of the present day'; also an appealing concertante-style Sonata Opus 167 by Saint-Saëns. Giacomo Setaccioli's Sonata Opus 31 (1921) is a stirring composition, though lengthy in places. Then follow works by Paul Juon (Opus 82, 1924), Jan Ingenhoven (1924), Siegfried Karg-Elert (Opus 139, 1924), and Woldemar von Bausznern (Instrumental Suite No. 3, 1924). Robert Bückmann wrote many pieces for wind instruments and had a particular aptitude for devising oboe music. He was responsible for the enchanting *Idylls* (MS, 1935), intended for pupils and amateur clarinettists, and a charming *Little Suite* (MS, 1935). Erich Sehlbach wrote some considerable compositions for clarinet and piano in *Musik* (MS, 1936) and *Fantasia* (MS, 1939). His work seeks to combine austere harmonies with polyphonic lines, and its effectiveness arises from the invention of lyric melodies and moods.

Honegger's little Sonatina for A clarinet is more widely known, particularly the sparkingly witty, somewhat jazz-like last movement (with glissando!) which is most effective. The Sonatina by Martinu is suitable for study purposes. Among the most important of recent sonatas is that by Paul Hindemith, which is not very demanding from the point of view of technique.

A very rewarding piece for the clarinettist is Günther Raphael's *Duck Sonatina*. In this, the humorous last movement is preceded by a little poem about a duck, which it illustrates. Among other

[1] Kornauth's Sonata Opus 3 was originally intended for viola and piano, for which it is more suitable than for clarinet and piano.

sonatas for clarinet and piano are those by R. d'Alessandro (Sonatina giocosa), the celebrated conductor Leonard Bernstein, Victor Bruns (Opus 22), F. Geissler (1954), F. F. Finke (1950), H. F. Hartig, E. B. Hill (Sonatina), D. G. Mason (1920), Darius Milhaud (Sonatina), H. Riethmüller (Opus 36), Jens Rohwer, W. Schneider (Sonatina), R. Schollum (Opus 55, Sonatina), H. Schlüter-Ungar (two Sonatas, Opus 112 and 114), J. Weinberger (Sonatina), H. Wirth, I. Hamilton and others.

Shorter pieces for clarinet and piano are by Busoni (Elegy), Hermann Zilcher, H. K. Schmid, Max Laurischkus, C. Clifton (Intermezzo and Humoresque, very effective), J. Driessler (5 Pieces Opus 24), B. Stevens, Reiner, Risinger (Puppet Suite), L. Weiner (Ballata), F. Wildgans (3 Recital Pieces), W. Heider (Dialogue I), Jürg Baur (Ballata Romana, 1960), Darius Milhaud (Caprice, Duo concertant), V. Pobjoy (4 Pieces), P. Rainer (Suite), M. Seiber (Pastorale). One of the most important works in this *genre* is Alban Berg's atonal Four Pieces (1913) where he incorporated special effects (*pppp* echo tones, flutter-tongue, *Klavierflageolett*).

Duets for two clarinets have been written (apart from works purely for practice and collections) by C. Lahusen (Fife Music), Aurelio Magnani (*Sei duetti da camera concertante*), W. Hess, Edward B. Hill, Gunther Schuller (clarinet and bass clarinet), W. Schneider (Partita).

Poulenc's Sonata for two clarinets, in B♭ and A, is technically demanding but effective. I. Ovalle wrote two Improvisations for two clarinets and bass clarinet. J. Pauer and A. Donato have composed for three clarinets; the latter also for four clarinets (Pastorale and Dance), as have T. B. Brown, Hovhaness (Divertimento Opus 61, 5), Alfred Uhl (Divertimento for three clarinets and bass clarinet), H. Jelinek (Divertimento for E♭, B♭, bass clarinets and basset horn, No. 8 in the twelve-tone work Opus 15).

Duets for clarinet and flute are by Ernst Krenek (Sonatina), Heitor Villa-Lobos (Choros), W. Burkhard (Serenade, difficult), and G. Migot (Suite), while duets with bassoon are by H. de Haan, Kurt Kunert (Opus 20, Sonata), J. P. Thilman, L. Fernandez (3 Invencos), Francis Poulenc (Sonata, difficult).

Duets with violin are attributable to Adolf Busch, Günther

Raphael (Chamber Music No. 6), Paul Hindemith; and J. N. David composed four Duets with viola (Op. 32).

Some noteworthy trios for clarinet, violin and piano have been written in recent years, notably Béla Bartók's *Contrasts*, composed to be performed by himself, the jazz clarinettist Benny Goodman and the violin virtuoso Joseph Szigeti. The violin and clarinet parts bristle with technical difficulties and can be performed only by first-class players (the clarinettist has to alternate between the A and B♭ clarinets, and the violinist is required to use a second violin in a different key for the opening of the third movement). Igor Stravinsky arranged the main items of his *Soldier's Tale* as a suite for this same instrumentation, and among other composers to write for it have been Aram Khachaturian (in the folklore manner), D. G. Mason, R. Walthew, Darius Milhaud, Ernst Krenek, H. Riethmüller.

Trios for clarinet, cello and piano are by Paul Juon (Trio miniature Opus 18, originally for violin but in 1914 arranged by the composer at the request of the Dahlke Trio), Alfred Uhl (Little Concerto), A. Hollander (Six Character Pieces in the form of a canon Opus 53).

Günther Raphael was responsible for a witty Trio for clarinet, cello and piano, and C. H. Grovermann, Vincent d'Indy, and Hermann Zilcher (Opus 90) wrote for the same instruments.

There is no room to deal here with typical classes of wind chamber music like quintets or the numerous trios for oboe, clarinet and bassoon, but some compositions with unusual instrumentations should be mentioned: Rudolf Jettel (Trio in C minor), and R. Kelterborn (Lyrical Chamber Music) for clarinet, violin and viola; H. Reger (Divertimento for flute and two clarinets), J. P. Thilman (Trio piccolo for alto flute, viola and bass clarinet), T. Blum (Trio for clarinet, violin and cello, 1928), Jan Ingenhoven (Pieces for flute, clarinet and harp), Alfred Swan (Trio for flute, clarinet and piano); H. Jelinek (*Vier kleine Kammermusiken* Opus 9) and W. Eisenmann have written for two clarinets and bassoon.

K. Schiske composed music for clarinet, trumpet and viola; I. Markevitch a Serenade for violin, clarinet and bassoon; Villa-Lobos (*Fantaisie*) and K. Roetscher for clarinet, bassoon and piano.

Adolf Busch's *Deutsche Tänze* for clarinet, violin and cello are pleasing and not too difficult.

The traditional quartet instrumentation of clarinet, violin, viola and cello has been adhered to by S. W. Müller in the Chamber Music Opus 1, H. Eder and Otto Färber in the Quartet Opus 15. Other combinations were tried by Heinrich Kaminski (Quartet Opus 1b for piano, clarinet, viola and cello), Ernst Reinstein (*Musik* for flute, clarinet, violin and piano), Arthur Honegger (Rhapsody for two flutes, clarinet and piano), R. Wagner-Regeny (Divertimento, 1954, for flute, clarinet, bassoon and percussion), Ferdinand Scherber (Quartet for oboe, clarinet, bass clarinet and piano). Paul Hindemith's Quartet for clarinet, violin, cello and piano is important but not easy to perform.

Quintets for clarinet and string quartet have been written by Herbert Howells (Rhapsody Quintet), J. Holbrooke (Opus 27, 1 and 2), Ewald Straesser, Franz von Hoesslin, S. W. Müller (Divertimento), Egon Kornauth, Joseph Lederer, R. Delaney, Theo Goldberg, Oscar von Hemel, Gordon Jacob, G. Landré, Johannes Thilman, W. Wordsworth, Ilse Fromm-Michaels (*Musica larga*), Karl Höller, and others. An outstanding work is Paul Hindemith's Quintet, in the second movement of which the player has to change from the B♭ to the E♭ clarinet. Günther Raphael wrote a Serenade for clarinet and string quartet.

The following composed quintets for clarinet, horn, violin and cello: Z. Fibich, R. Kahn and W. von Bausznern. J. M. Hauer, I. Labor and F. Weingartner wrote quintets for clarinet, string trio and piano.

Prokofiev wrote an Overture on Yiddish themes for clarinet, string quartet and piano. A Sextet by K. Schiske is for the same instrumentation, and J. Engel wrote Suite No. 1 for clarinet and string quartet.

Unusual instrumentations are to be found in Arnold Schönberg's Suite Opus 29 for E♭ clarinet, B♭ clarinet, bass clarinet, violin, viola, cello and piano; in Hindemith's Septet for flute, oboe, clarinet, bass clarinet, bassoon, horn and trumpet (1948); Martinu's Serenade for two clarinets and string trio; Prokofiev's Quintet for oboe, clarinet, violin, viola and double bass; Casella's Serenata for clarinet, bassoon and string trio; and Carl Nielsen's Serenata for clarinet, horn, bassoon, cello and double bass.

Lieder and songs with solo clarinet have been composed more often. Thus, Armin Knab wrote *Five Hungarian Folk Songs* for three female voices, clarinet and piano, an instrumentation which follows the pattern set by Schubert, and Ewald Straesser composed the *Geistliche Gesänge* Opus 57 for medium voice, clarinet and organ. Altogether novel combinations were tried by Heinrich Kaminski in three religious *Lieder* for voice, clarinet, and violin, Erich Sehlbach in the *Wildgans Sonnets* for baritone, clarinet and viola (MS, 1931), Hermann Simon in three sparkingly witty songs *Vom Kinderparadies* (1939) for medium voice, clarinet and cello, and Igor Stravinsky in the curious *Berceuses du chat* for female voice, E♭, A (and B♭) and bass clarinets (1916).

Anton Webern wrote many songs with instrumental accompaniment, e.g. five Canons for soprano, clarinet and bass clarinet; three Folk Texts, Op. 17, for voice, violin, clarinet and bass clarinet; three *Lieder* Opus 18 for guitar and clarinet. M. Seiber composed three *Morgenstern Lieder* for soprano and clarinet; Copland has written for soprano, flute and clarinet; H. Heiss for soprano, clarinet and piano (*Kästner Aphorisms*); Dallapiccola for voice and three clarinets (*Goethe Lieder*); Stravinsky, apart from the *Berceuses du chat*, three songs by Shakespeare for mezzosoprano, flute, clarinet and viola.

Among the most important recent solo concertos are the beautiful Clarinet Concerto for A clarinet in four movements by Hindemith (for Benny Goodman); the Concerto by Milhaud, who also wrote a Concerto for flute, clarinet, violin and viola; a Concerto by Aaron Copland, commissioned by Benny Goodman (with string orchestra, harp and piano, in two movements with a virtuoso solo cadenza in the middle; the first movement slow and emotional, the second quick with jazz elements); and the Concertino by M. Seiber. It is a matter of regret that Richard Strauss's Concertino for clarinet, bassoon and string orchestra with harp is so rarely performed these days. It is a lovable work of the aged master. A Concerto for clarinet and bassoon by Martelli is of little significance.

Among further noteworthy works are the Concertos by J. Rivier, Bloch, Nielsen; *Atonalyse I* for clarinet and strings by Karl Günther

Breuer, the Arioso for clarinet and string orchestra by Otto Abel von Sosen, the Clarinet Concerto by V. Bruns, Krenek's Suite for clarinet and strings, the Elegy by H. Wennig, and the pleasing Serenade for flute, clarinet and string orchestra by Conrad Beck.

The *Ebony Concerto* by Stravinsky, written for the ebony clarinet of Woody Herman and his band, is not a clarinet concerto in the strict sense of the word but a piece for jazz band in which the first clarinet takes the leading part.

THE CLARINET IN THE ORCHESTRA

Although the preceding chapters dealt mainly with solo and chamber music literature for the clarinet it will be remembered that the instrument is of greater importance in the orchestra than in concertos and chamber music. In wind bands the clarinet takes the leading role,[1] and in light music it holds a dominant position among the woodwind, owing not so much to its technical potentialities as to its special qualities in tone and compass. No other woodwind possesses a compass of more than three and a half octaves or a tone as incisive and yet as capable of modulation, and as intimate as the clarinet. And if unalterable acoustic properties make its technical mastery difficult, yet they render the clarinet sufficiently flexible to satisfy any demands: as a rule, orchestral parts for the clarinet have more notes in their various passages than those for oboe and bassoon.[2]

Gevaert, an outstanding connoisseur of instruments, writes in

[1] In this connection, the important role of the clarinet in jazz music should not be overlooked, although it was more pronounced in the early days of jazz than it is today. In the 'classical' jazz era it was along with cornet or trumpet, the foremost instrument to carry the tune, but it was more or less superseded by the saxophone with its greater volume, and today it is found mainly in bands of the traditional styles, especially New Orleans but also Chicago and Swing. The main function of the clarinet lies in the frisky figuration, especially in the high register. The glissando is a popular effect, produced by a particular method of blowing. In jazz the B♭ clarinet is the favourite instrument.

[2] Towards the end of the last century, Professor Gustave Poncelet, clarinet teacher at the Brussels Conservatory, experimented with an orchestra consisting of two E♭, five first, four second and four third B♭ clarinets, four basset horns and six bass clarinets, a contra-basset horn and a contrabass clarinet. Poncelet toured Belgium with this clarinet orchestra and even performed, amongst other works, the *Lohengrin* prelude and symphonies by Mozart. Wilhelm Altenburg was very impressed by these concerts (ZfI. 19, p. 122), and the orchestra inspired the formation of playing groups of clarinettists in England and America; Robert Stark organised similar concerts in Würzburg.

his *Traité général d'instrumentation*: 'No wind instrument offers to the composer such manifold technical possibilities as the clarinet. We know already its wide compass and diverse tone colours. No less remarkable are its flexibility in the expression of dynamic nuances. Its tone is soft, yet incisive; the clarinet is better than oboe and bassoon in the crescendo and decrescendo to the ultimate limits of pianissimo. Where necessary, it is also capable of a more rapid articulation. Finally, it adjusts itself admirably to the various forms of musical thought: an expressive interpreter of solemn song, the clarinet deals easily and naturally with fluent passages, so long as they are not too far removed from its most usual keys.' The most brilliant master of the art of instrumentation, Richard Strauss, said of the clarinet: 'More than any other woodwind, it is capable of all dynamic graduations from the faintest *pp* to the shrillest *ff*, and can thus transmit to the listeners' senses the finest nerve vibrations in the beautifully articulated body of the modern orchestra.'

From its introduction into the orchestra, the clarinet has generally been used in pairs, Wagner specified three clarinets as well as a bass clarinet for the first time in *The Ring*. Richard Strauss had a particular preference for wind instruments, and among them especially favoured the clarinet family. In his stage works, he employed the following instruments of this group:

Salome (1905)   1 E♭, 2 A, 2 B♭ clarinets, 1 bass clarinet
Elektra (1909)   1 E♭, 2 A, 2 B♭ clarinets, 2 basset horns, 1 bass clarinet
Der Rosenkavalier (1911)   1 part (i.e. one player) for D, E♭, A and B♭ clarinets; 2 parts for A, B♭, and C clarinets; 1 part for bass clarinet and basset horn
Josephslegende (1914)   1 D, 2 A, bass and contrabass clarinets
Die Frau ohne Schatten (1921)   1 E♭, 2 B♭, 2 C clarinets, 2 basset horns, 1 bass clarinet

Until the middle of the last century, the technique of clarinet playing received the most valuable impulses through the medium of the solo concerto; then, when wind-instrument virtuosi fell out of favour, the empahsis shifted to operatic and symphonic scores. At the present time, the technique of the clarinettist has reached a pitch which can hardly be surpassed unless the mechanism of the clarinet comes to be completely revolutionised by new inventions.[1] For this enormous technical improvement, which no player or instrument maker could have foreseen, we must thank Richard Strauss. His magnificent intuition for the character and thorough knowledge of the technical potentialities of the clarinet enabled the master to inspire refinements, as to the same extent in all other instruments. While in the previous decades composers long since forgotten had made excessive demands on the player and really asked for the impossible, Strauss always recognised the limits. It is not too much to say that, given sufficient study, even his most difficult figures can be played. Of course, the tempo plays a decisive role! Even a trifling increase in speed may often render an otherwise quite feasible passage impossible (in *Guntram* Strauss even demands an attack on *c''''*).

As a special effect, Strauss specified the flutter-tonguing (in *Don Quixote*, to illustrate the bleating of sheep) which recently has invaded even light operatic scores (Robert Stolz, *Himmelblaue Träume*). Unfortunately, so far most German clarinettists strive in vain to master this difficult tongue action, just as they only rarely manage a convincing execution of the 'double tonguing' which is occasionally required, though in the Latin countries clarinettists are often very proficient in these complicated tongue techniques. The reason may lie in some physiological considerations, but lack of practice is at least partly responsible.

Flutter-tonguing is produced like a lingual *r*, as spoken, for instance, by the Italians, in which the tip of the tongue 'flutters'

[1] The enormous perfection of the clarinet technique is best illustrated by the fact that of all the clarinettists in Berlin in the first half of the last century, F. W. Tausch alone was able to master the clarinet run in the *Chaos* introduction to the *Creation* (Schreiber, p. 172). In this connection, it should be noted that not every wind-instrument virtuoso was also an outstanding orchestral player. The Journal *Das Orchester* wrote in 1850 about a famous clarinet virtuoso who had been asked to play in the orchestra at the Lower Rhine Music Festival in Cologne. Before the final rehearsal he indulged in 'the most famous roulades', including the note E in five octaves. 'No sooner had the oratorio started than it transpired that our brave virtuoso was at his wit's end; having thrown the whole orchestra into the loveliest confusion and brought it to the verge of utter disaster, he stole away from his stand, packed up his precious clarinet, and was never seen again' (Schreiber, p. 90).

against the front part of the roof of the mouth. Alban Berg used this effect frequently. Like double and triple tonguing, it is easier to execute on the flute.

Double and triple tonguing (ti–ke, ti–ke and ti–ti–ke or ti–ke–ti respectively) allows of a more rapid, though somewhat less exact staccato than the simple tongue stroke.

The glissando is frequently heard in jazz music (e.g. the famous solo at the opening of Gershwin's *Rhapsody in Blue*). A really satisfactory glissando can be produced only in the overblown register (from *b'*) and then only in an ascending scale. The glissando results from a slow sliding away of the fingers from the tone-holes and a special kind of embouchure (thus, in playing an ascending slur, e.g. *g"–c'''*, one may try not to change the embouchure at *c'''*, which is normally automatic; one soon learns to sustain the tone and slowly to press it upwards, though for this exercise, the reed should not be too strong). Muting (placing a cloth in the bell) has little effect with the clarinet (in contrast to the conical saxophone). It merely modifies the notes produced from the holes near the bell. Stravinsky occasionally specifies this effect but it is not often used.

At the time of their introduction into the orchestra, the main instruments in the clarinet family were the A, B♭ and C clarinets; for a time, though very rarely, the B natural clarinet was also in use.[1] After the refinements introduced by Ivan Müller and H. E. Klosé, the C clarinet lost its importance because of its incisive tone, and at present it is used only for specific purposes, so that the A and B♭ clarinets dominate scores. Wind bands have also dropped the A clarinet, using, apart from the big and small clarinets, only the B♭ instrument.

The C clarinet, the only non-transposing member of this large family, has a lively, brilliant tone. Some earlier and more recent composers have therefore employed it to characterise rural and peasant scenes. Typical examples are in *Der Freischütz* (Peasant March in Act I), *The Bartered Bride* and *Der Rosenkavalier*. But although C clarinet parts are frequently found in the general

---

[1] Mozart specified the B natural clarinet in *Idomeneo* and *Così fan tutte* (the parts transposed for A in the printed score), and M. Carafa in *Nozze di Lucia di Lammermoor*. In 1831 Brod supplied a B clarinet to the Paris Opera (Sachs, *Reallexikon*).

literature of older operatic and symphonic music, as well as in lighter works, in practice the instrument is rarely used, and its parts are usually transposed by the player. This is fully justified since, as we know today, the classical masters specified the C clarinet not because of its shrill tone but in spite of it, for purely technical reasons. At the time of the Viennese classics, the clarinet had no more than five or six keys and its fingering was considerably more complicated than that of any other woodwind. For that reason, instruments in different keys had to be used in order to satisfy the demands of the different tonalities employed by the composer. The C clarinet served in the keys of C, G and F; otherwise the Bb clarinet for the flat keys, and the A clarinet for the sharp keys. That is the reason why the old masters specified the C clarinet in places where, to our ears, it is quite unsuitable (e.g. Beethoven, Leonora Overture No. 3), and such parts are rightly transposed today.[1] Occasionally, however, the use of the C clarinet is due to a certain carelessness, particularly among Italian composers.[2] Regardless of key, they almost invariably specified the C clarinet and left the players to do the necessary transposing.

On the other hand, the C parts of more recent composers who deliberately specify C clarinets because of their tone colour (e.g. Berlioz in the Witches' Sabbath in *Symphonie fantastique*, where C and Eb clarinets are specified), should not be played on the Bb clarinet. Clarinettists are usually good at transposing and prefer to play the parts on the instruments they are accustomed to, even though C clarinets may be available. (A parts are occasionally played on Bb clarinets with low Eb keys, and in the orchestral studies by R. Temple Savage all passages for A and C clarinets are accompanied by their transpositions for Bb clarinets.)

[1] Verdi, too, often choose the clarinets according to the key of his composition. In the Azucena aria No. 5 in *Il Trovatore* he specified the C clarinet, although it meant inferior tone: in bars 19–20 of the part in 6/8 time, he scored for the first clarinet and the low instruments of the orchestra the important sequence *f♯* to *g*, and repeated this motif in the next two bars a minor third lower; but the clarinet is omitted from the repetition because it cannot reach the lowest note, which, however, is available on the Bb clarinet. Since clarinettists transpose this aria in any case, they often put in the (sounding) *d♯/e* of bars 21–22 and thus remove an obvious tonal anomaly.

[2] In recent years some makers have produced C clarinets which are played with a Bb mouthpiece.

Before the first performance of *Der Rosenkavalier*, Richard Strauss wrote a letter to the conductor, Ernst von Schuch, in which he said: 'The C clarinets are indispensable, urge you to get some. Transposition impossible.' But the instruments specifically purchased for this performance were never used again because the players preferred their B♭ clarinets. Strauss was furious and wrote a strong letter to the orchestra management in Dresden which 'they wouldn't have liked at all' (Kunitz). Subsequently, Strauss repeatedly specified the C clarinet (*Die Frau ohne Schatten, Die ägyptische Helena, Arabella, Friedenstag, Daphne, Die Liebe der Danae, Capriccio*). Where C-instruments are available (good ones!) they should certainly be used. Mahler also deliberately specified the C clarinet.

It should be added that C clarinets by good makers do not have the vulgar, coarse tone constantly referred to in literature, although they naturally sound somewhat brighter and less smooth. Their very characteristic tone colour cannot be simulated by either B♭ or E♭ clarinets.

Better known than this clarinet is its little sister in E♭, which has been at home in Prussian military bands since 1805–6 and today numbers from one to three in almost every wind band. It has also played a considerable part in symphonic and operatic orchestras ever since Hector Berlioz used it in his *Symphonie fantastique* (1830–31), and Richard Strauss, as well as other contemporary composers, employed its piercing tone and its shrill, often grotesque effect. Moreover, for many decades the E♭ clarinet, together with the F clarinet,[1] was the favourite conducting instrument of bandmasters in the German infantry, until in the 1860s it was replaced by the baton. The compass of this very flexible instrument extends up to the written g''', sounding $b'''♭$, though today a skilful player may reach even higher notes.

As well as Strauss, many recent composers (Ravel, Mahler, Stravinsky, Schönberg and many others) have used the E♭ clarinet and given it solo passages.

[1] Already in the 1830s, the F clarinet was declining in importance. It is said that about 1810 it replaced the oboe, often missing in military bands. Beethoven and Mendelssohn specified it in their marches. For a short time, there were also clarinets in high E, high G and high A.

28 Heinrich Josef Baermann
(1784–1847)

29 Carl Baermann
(1811–1885)

30 Johann Simon Hermstedt
(1778–1846)

31 Joseph Friedlowsky
(1777–1859)

Very similar in tone is the somewhat more softly-coloured D clarinet. In the eighteenth century this was an important and frequently used tonality for which Molter wrote four concertos and for which parts also occur in operatic scores (e.g. J. C. Bach's *Orione*). It never completely disappeared. Cherubini used it in *Démophoon*, Liszt in *Mazeppa*, and Wagner in *Tannhäuser* and the *Valkyries* where, together with piccolo and harp, the D clarinet represents the dancing flames of the *Feuerzauber* music. In the original scores of valses by Lanner and Strauss the first clarinet is often pitched in D or Eb according to the tonality of the piece. In more recent years it has been specified by Mahler, Schönberg, Bartók and others, but particularly by Richard Strauss who specifies it in *Till Eulenspiegel* for the merry fool's motif of the title role.

D pitch is demanded much less often than Eb, but as a rule the larger operatic and symphonic orchestras possess Eb and D clarinets, played with the same mouthpiece. Otherwise D parts are played on the Eb clarinet. The D clarinet plays no part in band music. Its compass corresponds to that of Eb clarinet, though in *Till Eulenspiegel* Strauss demands the written $a'''b$, sounding $b'''b$.

With a length of about 15 inches, the Ab clarinet is the smallest in regular use today. It was never very well-known and for years generally forgotten, only gipsy musicians using it, though brilliantly. It was introduced into the band of the Royal Bavarian Infantry Guards in 1839 and then in several other South German and Austrian military bands, but it probably did not prove very useful and was discarded. On the other hand, it has played a more important part in Italy, and Verdi specified it in the scores for the large stage-bands of some of his operas (e.g. *La Traviata*). The instrument was also known and popular in Belgium. In the great miners' band of Brussels, the 'Harmonie de la Bouverie', there were three of them. The compass of this shrill and piercing instrument corresponds roughly to that of the flute, comprising the written scale $e'-f''''$, sounding $c'-d''''b$.

Small clarinets in high Bb, C and Eb are extremely rare but have apparently been used occasionally. No parts for them are known but the Instrument Museum in Brussels possesses a Bb clarinet of about 13 inches in length, and an Italian work on instrumentation, published in 1850, mentions a high C clarinet. A small E♭ clarinet was used as a substitute for a missing piccolo in connection with the 'Janissary music' (Schreiber, p. 169).

Today study works form an essential part of clarinet literature, but they were written comparatively late and until the beginning of the nineteenth century would-be clarinettists had to be content with very primitive material. Instructions of how to teach oneself to play the clarinet existed in the first half of the eighteenth century (e.g. by Eisel and Majer)[1] but were of extremely poor quality. Proper 'Methods' and 'Instructions' for the clarinet did not appear before the end of the century and, compared with modern works, they could not satisfy any but the most modest requirements. These tutors commonly opened with somewhat verbose and not very clear or precise introductions, explaining the clarinet and methods of making reeds and giving some hints on embouchure and how to hold the instrument; then followed some rather naive remarks about musicians and music in general and an explanation of the notes; finally, there were some primitive exercises and duets which did not convey any very clear picture of the method.

One of the earliest tutors was probably that by Abrahame, who in 1788, at the age of 22 (?) was employed as *maître de clarinette* at the Opéra in Paris. Schilling praised the work and called it excellent; unfortunately, it is not to be found in any library, so that his opinion cannot be verified. Another tutor which appears to have been lost, was *Nouvelle Méthode de Clarinette* (1796) by Frédéric Blasius,[2] a German from the Lower Rhineland, who worked at the

---

[1] For the different fingering methods recommended by Eisel and Majer, see H. Becker in *Mf.* VIII, 1955, pp. 271 ff.

[2] A clarinet tutor preserved by the Paris Conservatoire is possibly attributable to Blasius.

Opéra Comique in Paris.[1] The *Neue theoretisch-praktische Klarinette-Schule nebst einer kurzen Abhandlung über das Basset-Horn* was published in 1803. Its author was the very versatile musician J. H. G. Backofen.[2] His little work was intended for the five-key clarinet and became outdated when Ivan Müller's important inventions came into prominence. Therefore, Backofen revised his tutor in 1824 and republished it under the title *Anweisung zur Klarinette mit besonderer Hinsicht auf die in neuern Zeiten diesem Instrument beigefügten Klappen*. . . . Its theoretical and practical content had been considerably expanded and a large fingering chart added. In England, *A new and complete Preceptor for the Clarinet . . . to which is added the gamut for the Clara Voce or Corno bassetto,* by John Mahon appeared in 1803, and in 1826–27 *A Complete Instruction Book for the Clarinet* by the famous virtuoso T. L. Willman.

Jean-Xavier Lefèvre's *Méthode de Clarinette* was published in 1802 and remained popular for many years. On 144 folio pages the celebrated clarinettist gave a thorough explanation of the instrument, embouchure, tone production and phrasing, followed by detailed instructions in elementary music. The practical section contained useful exercises, mostly in the form of duets, and, finally, some 'sonatas' of several movements for two clarinets which were not too easy to play on the simple contemporary instruments, though generally in easy keys. At a committee meeting of members of the Paris Conservatoire the manuscript was highly praised and officially adopted. Although it cannot satisfy all modern requirements, it is still in use. A German edition, edited and enlarged by Hermann Bender,[3] appeared some 60 or 70 years ago and is also still used occasionally. Although Bender made some sweeping changes, essential parts were retained. Lefèvre's tutor is also in use in Italy as edited and translated by the well-known clarinettist Romeo Orsi. In 1939, A. Giampieri published a revised Italian edition. The Czech *Skola pro Klarinet* by Julius Pisarowic is essentially based on Lefèvre's 140-years-old tutor.

As the clarinet continued to improve, tutors had to keep pace,

[1] One of the oldest preserved tutors (Paris, 1795) was written by A. Vanderhagen.
[2] Backofen travelled as a clarinet and basset horn virtuoso, later worked as flautist and bassoonist, and was also an excellent player of the pedal harp.
[3] Bender also published his own clarinet tutor.

and when Ivan Müller had invented the 13-key clarinet, he immediately published a tutor dedicated to the King of England, which was republished several times in German and French. In 1836 when Müller's improvements had finally been accepted in France, Frédéric Berr wrote a new comprehensive tutor for the 14-key clarinet which had meanwhile come on the market. It largely replaced Lefèvre's outdated work and is still in use in France in a reprint edited by Mimart. Among other authors of clarinet tutors were Franz Thaddäus Blatt (Prague), Joseph Küffner, Joseph Fröhlich, and J. Fahrbach (Vienna, 1840, for a 19-key clarinet).

All these tutors had to be abandoned or re-edited when Buffet and Klosé invented the so-called Boehm clarinet. The invention was not patented until 1844 but in the preceding year Klosé published an excellent, comprehensive tutor for the new clarinet, which soon began to replace Berr's work. An extremely efficient revision of Klosé's tutor, in which many well-known French clarinettists collaborated, was published in 1933. Klosé's work was here extended by numerous modern exercises for beginners and advanced études, in addition to an appendix containing orchestral studies. It now represents a study volume adapted to modern techniques and well able to accompany the clarinettist from the first stage to maturity and beyond. However, in Germany the tutor is not in common use because it is adapted to the Boehm system. A tutor for both systems was written by Romero y Andia (1860), and H. Lazarus' tutor appeared in London in 1881.

But Germany also has some excellent clarinet tutors, the best-known and most widely used being Carl Baermann's comprehensive work. Dedicated to Duke Ernst of Saxe-Coburg-Gotha, this *Vollständige Clarinett-Schule von dem ersten Anfange bis zur höchsten Ausbildung des Virtuosen* appeared in five volumes from 1864–1875, with two volumes of piano accompaniments to the *Salonstücke* (salon pieces) contained in it. An enlarged edition, also available in English and French, was published in 1917–18 by the famous Berlin clarinettist Oskar Schubert who died in 1935. Under his editorship it grew to 10 volumes, with three additional books of orchestral studies. In general, Schubert's editing consisted in the correction of some imprecise or unclear passages, an alteration in the fingering brought into line with progress in the construction of clarinets, and the supplementation of the exercises by new scales and chord exercises and some staccato études.

Another German clarinet tutor of outstanding merit is the *Grosse theoretisch-praktische Clarinett-Schule . . . nebst Anweisung zur Erlernung des Bassetthorns und der Bassclarinette* by Robert Stark. It appeared in 1892 in two parts with German and English text, as Opus 49. A third volume *Die Hohe Schule des Clarinettspiels*, Opus 51, appeared eight years later. It contains 24 great exercises of virtuoso standard.

A greater contrast than that between the works of Baermann and Stark can hardly be imagined. Baermann's musical perception had its roots largely in the glittering era of virtuosity; he provides technical exercises only where they seem quite indispensable and tries to make the lesson as inspiring and entertaining as possible through musically compact descriptive pieces, the so-called *Salon-stücke*. On the other hand, Stark proceeds very differently; he makes no concessions to the learner and provides exclusively technical exercises and études, interspersing them only with one sonata for two clarinets and one for two clarinets and a basset horn. A regrettable prejudice on the part of many clarinettists has led to a certain rivalry between the protagonists of Baermann on the one hand, and of Stark on the other, although it is quite wrong to concentrate on one method to the exclusion of the other. Used properly, the two works complement each other very happily and should both be employed in the training of professional musicians. Baermann's compositions introduce the pupil to the elements of good tone production and of expression, in short, to all the necessary musical refinements, while Stark's exercises perfect his fingering and tongue technique.

Apart from these outstanding works, there are many bigger and smaller tutors offering valuable material for the training of amateur clarinettists and even the would-be professional player. For the basic principles it is perhaps often advisable to turn to one of these smaller works, since both Baermann and Stark deal rather cursorily with the first beginnings. In the first place, there are three works by Dresden clarinettists. The oldest, by Friedrich Demnitz, still has something to offer but is outmoded in its structure and so scanty as to make it suitable only for amateurs. The professional beginner should turn to a tutor by Maximilian Gabler (1906), who adopted some of the features of Baermann's work, while in Hermann Lange's tutor (1911) the main emphasis is on solid technical foundations. Neither of these works can lead the musician to artistic maturity but, as H. Lange states in his preface, if he makes full use of the instructions, he will gain a sound knowledge of his art.

A tutor for the German and Boehm clarinets, published in 1940, by the Gera chamber music virtuoso H. Melotte (dedicated to Heinrich XLV, hereditary Prince of Reuss) seeks and applies completely new methods. Strictly systematically, the pupil is taken step by step from the very beginning to full mastery, though willpower and persistence are indispensable requisites for a successful use of this novel tutor.

Apart from these main German works, there are good clarinet tutors in other languages. Several appeared in Czechoslovakia, the most successful among them a work in two volumes by Stanislav Krtička[1] (1939). A tutor by Frederick Thurston and Alan Frank was published in London in the same year and, like those by G. Langenus (1913) and E. Gay (1932), is intended for the Boehm clarinet. The Italian *La scuola del bel canto italiano* (1929) by Alessandro Cardoni is really a collection of popular Italian opera arias arranged for clarinet and piano and does not keep the promise of its title. Ferdinando Busoni, the father of Ferrucio Busoni (1883), also wrote a clarinet tutor. More recent works are by Rudolf Jettel (very thorough and comprehensive but dry), Robert Kietzer (short, suitable for band music), Willy Schneider, W. Hofmann (both of the latter fairly short but suitable for elementary lessons and younger pupils), Artie Shaw, Benny Goodman (both chiefly for jazz), R. Willaman, O. Schmal, R. Gräfe, and G. Balassa in collaboration with K. Berkes.

[1] Stanislav Krtička was for many years professor at the Brno State Conservatory, previously in Zagreb. In addition to many other works, he published a small *Folk Clarinet School* (1925) in the Czech and Croat languages, as well as some valuable studies about the clarinet and its literature. Foremost among these publications was *Wegweiser beim Unterricht der Klarinette* (in German and Czech, 1936; with comprehensive bibliography for clarinet, saxophone and tarogato) and *Péče o Plátek* (troubles with the clarinet reed) (1937, now out of print).

Soon after the publication of the first clarinet tutors, some of the best musicians recognised the need for more practice material and for this purpose wrote études and caprices. Though the earliest of these collections, by Abrahame and Michel Yost, have apparently been lost, many of those written only a little later or about the middle of the century by other composers are still available. Among them, the collections by Ivan Müller and Heinrich Baermann are chiefly suitable for beginners, while Hyacinthe Klosé's books of études, re-edited by Paul Jeanjean, make greater demands, especially the caprices by J. B. Gambaro. The scale exercises by Frédéric Berr, also re-edited by P. Jeanjean, are little known outside France. In Italy use is still made of études by Lefèvre and J. B. Gambaro, both revised by A. Giampieri, and by F. T. Blatt.

Among later collections of études of the last century are some by Luigi Bassi, Ernesto Cavallini, Georges Haseneier, E. Krakamp, Fritz Kroepsch, Guiseppe Marasco, Robert Stark, Heinrich Wahls and L. Wiedemann. Outstanding among these works are the caprices by Cavallini and the études by Stark and Kroepsch. Benedetto Carulli and D. Mirco have published exercises based on piano études by Henry Bertini (*le jeune*).

The increasingly greater demands made by more recent composers on the fingering skill of players have led to the publication of many more volumes of exercises. In particular, French clarinettists and teachers concerned themselves with the extension of study material and wrote numerous considerable works. Outstanding among these are études by A. Périer, clarinet professor at the Paris Conservatoire (*Enseignement complet*, five books, 1931–32), as well as the books by Paul Jeanjean (*Vademecum du clarinettiste*, 1927: *Etudes progressives et mélodiques*, three books, 1928–29) and Gaston Hamelin (*Gammes et exercises*, 1930). In 1937 the clarinettist and bandmaster Henry Sarlit published *Zwanzig Primavista-Etüden für zwei Klarinetten* based on pieces by old masters. He had previously published *25 Virtuosen-Studien nach Werken von Chopin and Schumann*. Both works are available with German text.

Innumerable French composers, past and present, have written *pièces de concours* (diploma pieces), among them Pierné, Bozza, Tomasi, Menager, Montbrun, d'Ollone and Rabaud.

In Italy, too, well-known musicians strove to reform and supplement existing exercises and wrote many new clarinet études. Among those of high quality known to the author are the books by Professor Alamiro Giampieri of Genoa (*14 Studi giornalieri*, 1935; *12 Studi moderni*, 1936; *6 Capricci*, 1937), occasionally reminiscent of Cavallini, and *Dodici grandi studi* (1928) by Antonio d'Elia. Also useful for study purposes are études by Gabucci, Thurston, Mercadante, Bertini and others. Among German études worth mentioning are those by the Vienna clarinettist Rudolf Jettel and by the composer Alfred Uhl, both of which satisfy every demand of contemporary music and are capable of perfecting the clarinettist's technique to the limit of what is possible, as well as exercises by H. Bender and R. Kling.

Orchestral studies are no less important to the young musician than tutors and études, and are useful even to the experienced artist. The most numerous and most important collections of difficult and solo orchestral passages are to be found in Germany, where the idea of orchestral studies probably originated. Perhaps the earliest collection for the clarinet is one initiated by the horn virtuoso Friedrich Gumbert, which has recently been edited and greatly enlarged by the Leipzig clarinettist Professor Edmund Heyneck. It contains, in addition to compositions by various other masters, a comprehensive selection from works by Beethoven, Brahms, Wagner and Liszt. Some of the books have been revised by Paul Gloger and republished; unfortunately, they are not all available. Apart from these comprehensive collections, the brief but very thorough orchestral studies by the chamber musician F. Hinze of Weimar are widely used. The first volume deals with opera, the second with the concert repertory and the third with Richard Wagner's compositions. Another large and detailed collection by Professor Oskar Schubert has been published as part of the new edition of Baermann's tutor. It consists of a short appendix to the second volume of the tutor and three separate books, including one for the bass clarinet.

The Viennese clarinettist Professor Bartholomey, in 1910, compiled orchestral studies from the works of Richard Strauss, and two years later the Berlin chamber musician Carl Essberger published a selection in six volumes from the works of the same master. Both editions are excellent in the selection and arrangement of the various passages, and may with justification be called exemplary. Unfortunately, no additions have been made to Essberger's collection since *Der Rosenkavalier*.

The voluminous book of orchestral studies by Alamiro Giampieri (1936) is well able to hold its own among these many excellent German collections, whether in Italy or in Germany. Apart from compositions by the great German, French and Russian masters, it contains chiefly works from the Italian operatic and concert repertoires.

Peters has published orchestral studies from symphonic works by Strauss. The collection by R. Temple Savage (Boosey & Hawkes) contains passages from the concert repertoire only; the third volume is the most important since it deals with modern compositions.

Studies from works for band music are represented by only one collection, the old edition by Otto Schilling in four books, dealing exhaustively with the most difficult and, at one time, most popular works. The same author, in collaboration with F. Müller, published orchestral studies from light music, which, however, are almost completely outdated; in six volumes they contain a wealth of material from light music today almost totally forgotten.

Basset horn and alto clarinet

Basset horn and alto clarinet occupy a position between the soprano and bass clarinets. The two instruments are often confused and unfortunately, as a rule, makers do not distinguish them clearly. In fact, the basset horn has measurements quite different from the alto clarinet and, consequently, completely different tone colour. A genuine basset horn has a narrower bore, so that its utterance is not sensuous and warm like that of clarinets proper but duller and flatter. Moreover, the compass of the basset horn extends a third lower, through four so-called 'basset keys', thus reaching written *c*, while the alto clarinet extends only down to *e*. Finally, the basset horn is pitched in the key of F, the alto clarinet usually in the key of Eb.[1]

The history of the origin of the basset horn is somewhat confused. It was probably first made about 1770 by A. and M. Mayrhofer of Passau, and subsequently improved by T. Lotz of Pressburg. Some instrument collections (Nuremberg, Hamburg and a private owner in Düren) possess instruments made by the former master. They have a very striking form: two crescent-shaped, carved-out wooden halves are glued together and, as with a cornet, covered with black or brown leather. This tube, from the curved shape of which the instrument takes its name, terminates in the so-called 'book', (*Buch*), a small box enclosing three parallel passages[2] of the bore

---

[1] Exceptionally the alto clarinet is in F and the basset horn in Eb, and there have also been basset horns in G. Mozart's first draft for the Clarinet Concerto (K. 584b) contains a solo part for basset horn in G.

[2] In two basset horns by Mayrhofer the 'book' is differently arranged but they probably represent experiments to find better ways of bending the tube. The normal

leading to the metal bell. This rude construction was not conducive to good tone quality, and towards the end of the eighteenth century someone hit on the idea of connecting two straight and therefore cleanly-bored tubes by means of a wooden or ivory knee-joint to form an obtuse angle. But as early as the beginning of the nineteenth century completely straight basset horns, with or without the book, were constructed, and in some of these the bells were bent upwards.

Owing to the primitive state of instrument making, the earliest basset horns had only five keys and a basset key for the low *c*. The key for low *d* was added very early, reputedly by the brothers Stadler, and a little later the keys for *c♯* and *d♯*. Further development of the basset horn went hand in hand with the refinement of the clarinet. Modern basset horns usually resemble saxophones in shape (fig. 17); the fingering mechanism corresponds to that of the soprano clarinet, differing only in the addition of the basset keys, manipulated by the right thumb, which either overlap like scales or are arranged in two pairs, one opposite the other.

As early as the 1770s, the private orchestra of Princess Elizabeth in Freiburg had three basset horns at its disposal if required. Kirrstein played the basset horn '*en premier*' and the clarinet, Czerny the basset horn '*en basse*' or the bassoon, and Natauschek bassoon or basset horn '*en basse*' (L. Schiedermair, 'Die Oper an den badischen Höfen', *Sammelbände der Internationalen Musikgesellschaft*, XIV, 1912, p. 3). In Paris, in 1774, M. Valentin played 'sur le corno-bassetto ou contra-clarinette' (*Mercure de France*, April 1774).

The tone character of the basset horn is illustrated in Mozart's *Magic Flute*, where it expresses the solemn gravity of Sarasto, and in his *Requiem* with its sombre foreboding of death.[1] Mozart had a particular affection for the instrument and in *Titus* wrote a masterly solo (Vitellia's Rondo) for it, as well as some beautiful cantilenas in Constanze's aria in *Die Entführung* (No. 10, almost invariably

---

way is that described above. As noticed earlier, Mahon, in his tutor (1803) refers to the basset horn as *Clara Voce*.

[1] E. T. A. Hoffmann mentions the basset horn as an instrument of a highly romantic character in *Kater Murr*, where, at a garden party, a basset horn quartet in the distance plays a melancholy love song. In *Kreisleriana* he likens the sound of the basset horn to the scent of red carnations.

omitted) and a rarely sung aria in *Figaro*[1] which he composed after the completion of the score (see also p. 65). In a letter to Clara Schumann dated 25 November 1855, Johannes Brahms spoke of a performance of this aria: 'Second: aria by Mozart, sung by Frau Guhrau with the orchestra. To my great delight, she was accompanied by two basset horns which had been found after some difficulties. I think no instrument adapts itself so closely to the human voice as the basset horn, whose tone is almost midway between a cello (bassoon) and a clarinet.' Mozart also assigned rewarding passages to the instrument in various instrumental works, especially in the *Maurerische Trauermusik* (K. 477) and the B♭ major wind Serenade (K. 361). Particularly in the latter work, Mozart succeeded brilliantly in demonstrating the great versatility of the instrument. Other Mozart compositions for the basset horn have been mentioned already, as also Mendelssohn's *Konzertstücke*. Stadler wrote some shorter works for the basset horn for his own use, e.g. some very pleasant Trios for three basset horns, some with descriptive titles.

Beethoven employed the basset horn only once, in the virtuoso solo in the ballet of *Die Geschöpfe des Prometheus*. In later years the basset horn fell almost into complete oblivion, although towards the end of the eighteenth and at the beginning of the nineteenth century it had been extremely popular as a solo instrument and a fair number of basset horn virtuosi[2] undertook concert tours with the works of fashionable composers long since forgotten.

In recent years, Richard Strauss tried to revive interest in the instrument. He employed it for the first time in *Elektra* (1908); in later operas, *Der Rosenkavalier*, *Die Frau ohne Schatten*, *Daphne*, *Die Liebe der Danae*, he assigned an increasingly independent part to the basset horn, and in *Capriccio* (1942) it takes the position of a solo instrument. Despite such interesting examples of the treatment of the basset horn, few composers have followed suit (Converse,

---

[1] K. 577, 'Al desio, di chit t'adora', with two concertante basset horns, composed 1789 for the Vienna performance of *Figaro* to replace Susanna's aria No. 27.

[2] For example, Backofen, C. Baermann, K. F. Bauersachs, Beerhalter, Anton David, V. Springer, the brothers Stadler, Tausch, A. Vanderhagen. Bochsa, Danzi (Grande Sonata Opus 62), C. Rommel, G. A. Schneider, and others, wrote concertos and sonatas for basset horns.

van Dieren, Escher, Flothuis, Holbrooke, Sessions). The basset horn compositions in the appendix to Stark's clarinet tutor are suitable only for study purposes (Sonata for two clarinets and basset horn; Serenade for two clarinets, basset horn and bass clarinet).

It is a matter of regret that in more recent chamber music, the basset horn is rarely used (B. Tuthill, Intermezzo for two clarinets and basset horn; H. Jelinek, Divertimento for E♭ clarinet, clarinet, basset horn and bass clarinet; and very recently, Giselher Klebe, Bagatelles for basset horn, trombone, harp and tubular bells).

The alto clarinet forms the true link between the normal and the bass clarinet. As the sound of the basset horn was too feeble for the orchestras and military bands of the nineteenth century, an attempt was made to construct a genuine alto clarinet with a wider bore. Ivan Müller took some trouble with the instrument and composed for it. The alto clarinet is pitched sometimes in F, but usually in E♭ and, as mentioned already, extends to the low (written) *e* like a normal clarinet. It sounds stronger and fuller than the basset horn and responds more surely. (E♭ alto clarinets extending to *d*, sounding F, are also made, for the purpose of playing basset horn parts.)

The alto clarinet was occasionally employed in the nineteenth century (especially in France, e.g. by Saint-Saëns) and also used for the basset horn parts in Mozart's compositions, for instance, since the basset horn had gone out of favour. In military bands it occupied a special place, and in recent years, it has been used almost exclusively by bands. German air force bands have used alto clarinets since 1939. An unusual instance of its concert use is by Joseph Holbrooke in *Apollo and the Seaman*.

A renowned maker, Streitwolf of Göttingen, tried about 1830 to construct a *Kontra-Altklarinette* in E♭, an octave below the alto clarinet proper, and Wilhelm Heckel of Biebrich-am-Rhein built a *Kontra-Bassetthorn* in 1905. Despite the efforts of other makers (e.g. J. Albert of Brussels and Evette of Paris), such instruments were entirely unsuccessful. For a time in the nineteenth century military bands used 'baritone clarinets' but this may have been only another name for the alto clarinet or the basset horn.

Finally, mention should be made of a curious clarinet today found only in museums, the *clarinette d'amour* (fig. 16). It was probably constructed to correspond to the oboe d'amore and was usually in the keys of A♭ or F, sometimes in G or even B♭ (at the same pitch as the soprano clarinet).[1] It differed from the soprano and alto clarinets in that it had a pear-shaped bell—the so-called *Liebesfuss*—and it had a slightly curved metal socket below the mouthpiece. The shape of the bell was supposed to produce a mellower and softer tone but it can only so operate with fully or nearly closed finger-holes; any belief that it would influence notes produced from the upper joint proved unfounded.

The large number of specimens to be found in public and private collections shows that the instrument was popular towards the end of the eighteenth century but at the turn of the century it was already outmoded. The clarinette d'amour only played a transitory role as an instrument of the gentlemanly amateur and has left no impression on serious music; J. C. Bach alone used three clarinettes d'amour in his opera *Temistocle* (1772). In a performing edition of the Overture (Breitkopf & Härtel OB 3795, Wiesbaden, 1957, edited by Fritz Stein) the parts have been wrongly transposed (for two A clarinets and bass clarinet in A). The instruments were pitched in D, but in this edition it was evidently assumed that the three clarinettes d'amour, two of which are scored in treble clef and the third in bass clef, would all sound one note higher than written—an erroneous assumption, as shown by a later arrangement of this movement by Bach himself for a performance in London where no clarinettes d'amour were available. In fact, Bach used the same curious notation which was common in those days for the French horn and the basset horn; in treble clef the clarinette d'amour sounds one seventh lower than written, in bass clef one tone higher. (Where the Breitkopf edition is used, the two clarinet parts should be executed one octave lower; basset horns would probably be closer to the tone originally intended.) The third clarinette d'amour in its solo part is taken to written *c* (in bass clef, therefore, sounding *d*). Thus, it may be concluded that the instruments used for the first performance in Mannheim (1772) already

[1] The Brussels instrument collection possesses even a clarinette d'amour in C.

possessed a basset key for low *c* (unless the original specification was, in fact, for basset horns in D?).

Joseph Haydn also seems to have employed the clarinette d'amour. Hoboken lists three Trios for 'Clarinetto d'Amour in B, Violino e Basso' (Hob. IV, E♭ 1, E♭ 2 and B♭ 1). These little pieces of divertimento character are intended for an instrument in the same tonality as the normal B♭ clarinet. They appear in Breitkopf's 1781 catalogue ('III Trii da Haydn, a Clarinetto, Violino e B.'; the word 'd'amour' is omitted); and also in the *Thematisches Verzeichnis der sämmtlichen Compositionen von Joseph Haydn. Zusammengestellt von Alois Fuchs*, Vienna 1840. Today, only one copy appears to be extant (with many errors), to be found in Zittau.

Bass and contrabass clarinets

The bass clarinet was invented relatively late, at a time when clarinet virtuosi were at their height and the basset horn enjoyed general popularity. Today, operatic and symphonic orchestras are unthinkable without the instrument and it is in common use in large bands. However, in German wind bands, it failed to gain a foothold in spite of occasional trials by Prussian (1833) and Bavarian military bands. From 1939–40 the bass clarinet was used in German air force bands though it has been an important member of bands in other countries for very much longer. The famous Banda municipale in Venice and the little less renowned Banda fascista di Chieti of Barcelona have two bass clarinets in addition to the bassoons; the full complement of the excellent band of the Garde Républicaine in Paris includes three, and the Belgian Harmonie de la Bouverie five bass clarinets. This bass instrument with its lovely tone may also be found in British and Swiss bands.

Since the bass clarinet sounds an octave below the B♭ clarinet,[1] it has twice its length and correspondingly a considerably wider

---

[1] Strangely enough, the bass clarinet in A has also been and still is written for. Today the bass clarinet is invariably pitched in B♭; other pitches have to be transposed by the player. The bass clarinet in C is rarely specified (e.g. by Liszt).

32 Arnold Joseph Blaes
(caricature) (1814–1892)

33 Hyacinthe Eléonore
Klosé (1808–1880)

34 Ernesto Cavallini (1807–1874)

35 Antonio Romeroy Andia
(1815–1886)

bore. Hence the fingerholes are much wider apart and cannot be covered directly. Therefore various auxiliary mechanisms have to be supplied to transfer finger pressure to the keys. The resulting complication of the mechanism retarded the development of the bass clarinet. It required numerous experiments and many years of work by a great number of makers to evolve an instrument which could be readily adopted by orchestras. Thanks to its skilful use by Wagner who frequently specified it since *Lohengrin*,[1] and by Liszt, it rapidly gained a firm hold.

First attempts to construct a bass clarinet were undertaken in 1772 by Gilles Lot of Paris who made what was named a *basse-tube*.[2] But this was soon forgotten and in 1793, independently of Lot, the famous woodwind-maker Heinrich Grenser of Dresden invented the *Klarinettenbass* with a (presumably written) compass of *b–f'''*. In 1807 a watch-maker, Desfontenelles of Lisieux, built a bass clarinet which in the struggle against Adolphe Sax and after, was proclaimed by several experts as the predecessor of the saxophone, although in fact it only anticipated its shape, and like any real clarinet overblew a twelfth, not an octave. The somewhat rudely made instrument had seven very big holes and the surprisingly large number of 12 keys. Dumas of Paris, in the same year, built the *basse-guerrière*, later to develop into an instrument which for the first time could be used in operatic orchestras. Five years later, François Sautermeister of Lyons introduced his *basse-orgue*, a metal instrument folded like a bassoon and possessing a chromatic compass of over three octaves. The bass clarinet of the excellent maker G. Streitwolf of Göttingen was of the same shape. It was first built in 1829 and in its revised form of 1833 was a 19-key instrument with a compass of contra-*A'♭* to *f''*. In the same period, two bass clarinets were made in Italy. The earlier was probably a strangely hunched and curved instrument (fig. 18) by Nicolo Papalini of Chiaravalle Milanese (near Pavia); the second the bassoon-like *glicibarifono*

---

[1] At the first performance of *Lohengrin* in Weimar, the bass clarinet, together with cor anglais and harp, were omitted, these instruments not having been represented in the court orchestra (Schreiber, pp. 133, 135, 141).
[2] Rendall refers to instruments (Berlin 2810, Brussels 939) with only one and three keys respectively. Perhaps they were not meant to overblow (a kind of bass chalumeau?). Because of their crude construction, he believes them to have been made about 1750.

('sweet-low-sounder') by Catterino Catterini of Bologna, first heard in 1838 at the Teatro Communale in Modena, after which it soon disappeared from the scene.

After a recital at the Paris Conservatoire in 1807, Dumas' *basse-guerrière* was highly praised by Méhul, Cherubini and other teachers at the institution. Three years later, this 13-key bass clarinet was adopted by the band of the Imperial Guard but fell into disuse again soon afterwards because musicians could not be persuaded to abandon the fingering method of their six-key clarinet and to learn instead the technique of a somewhat more complicated instrument. In 1814 Dumas again resumed work on his bass clarinet and at his death (1832) bequeathed the invention to the clarinettist Dacosta, who finally made it a great success. Dacosta introduced a slightly improved version of the bass clarinet to the public and gained much recognition. The distinguished musicologist F. J. Fétis wrote as follows: 'At the sight of these large, even gigantic instruments, most listeners anticipated hard and rough sounds, instead of which they were regaled with the strong, full, yet mellow tones which M. Dacosta produced with the greatest ease and as rapidly, purely and clearly as if he were playing a soprano clarinet.' L. A. Buffet provided some further refinements, and in 1836 the instrument was used for the first time in Meyerbeer's opera *Les Huguenots*. The grand solo in the Fifth Act helped to make it known in the widest circles of musicians and amateurs.

In the meantime in Brussels, the brilliant maker Adolphe Sax had applied himself to the solution of the problems inherent in the construction of a bass clarinet. In the year of the debut of the Dumas-Dacosta bass clarinet, Sax concluded a long series of experiments and proceeded to build a straight instrument which proved so superior to Dacosta's that in later years the latter himself used Sax's bass clarinet. It was the perfection of this instrument which made possible the final adoption of the bass clarinet by orchestras everywhere. In Germany especially, it remained the model for most instruments up to today. As the soprano clarinet developed over the years, the key mechanism of the bass clarinet underwent changes too numerous to mention here.

The bass clarinet is the most expressive of the deep wind instruments and therefore better suited than any other to the performance of soloistic cantilenas. Wagner, in particular, made effective use of its soft, flexible tone, for instance, in the beautiful solo passages in *Tannhäuser* and, above all, in *Tristan und Isolde* (Marke's entry in the Second Act):

Unfortunately, there are few chamber music works, let alone solo pieces with orchestra, with dominating bass clarinet. To name some that are available, there are the very rewarding Sonata Opus 40 by Othmar Schoeck (with piano), a Romance by August Klughardt (with orchestra), and a Quintet by York Bowen (with string quartet). In addition, there are some smaller compositions by Diethe, K. R. Goepfart, G. Schuller (Duet with clarinet), Thilman (*Gestalten*, with piano, and *Trio piccolo* with alto flute and viola), and others, particularly *pièces de concours* by French composers.

Present-day bass clarinets are in B♭ and fingering is similar to that on the normal clarinets up to *c′′′* (above that fingering is different). In addition, there are two keys to be controlled by the right thumb for written *e♭* and *d* (fig. 21). The low *e♭* is necessary when parts written in A (e.g. in works by Wagner and Strauss) are transposed (earlier bass clarinets reached only *e*). Modern compositions occasionally demand *d* (e.g. Schoeck's Sonata). Some bass clarinets are made today which encompass *c* (sound: contra-B♭) like the basset horn, so that bassoon parts can be played on them. For the bass clarinet *c* is not often demanded (it is, e.g. by Khachaturian). The bass clarinet requires two speaker keys which, like the *b′♭* key, are controlled automatically by a thumb lever (according to fingering combination). As this mechanism is somewhat delicate and liable to go wrong, many players prefer a separate lever for the second speaker key.

It may be added here that such an automatic mechanism would

also be desirable for the ordinary clarinet. An additional hole for *b'♭* renders that note fuller and permits a better-tuned *e* and *f* (Grässel of Nuremberg builds clarinets with such mechanism). An additional speaker key would improve intonation and render more sonorous the 'long' *b'* and *c"*. But the automatic mechanism is too complicated, and if the two thumb levers were separate, the player would have to learn a new technique. Sax already had two speaker-keys on his clarinet but, in spite of undeniable merits, the idea has never succeeded, for the reasons stated.

Regrettably, there is no uniformity in the notation for the bass clarinet. The easiest from the player's point of view is the so-called French notation in treble clef a ninth too high, that is the written notes correspond to the same fingering as on the normal clarinet. The so-called German notation is in bass clef one tone too high, which is more difficult for the player, especially if he has to transpose parts written in A at the same time. Moreover, in the German notation, the high notes are written in treble clef to save ledger lines, and still one tone above the sound, which means in practice that the player has to do an octave transposition. To make matters worse, some composers (Rimsky-Korssakov) use the German method in the bass clef and the French method in the treble clef![1] Preferably, the French notation should be used, at least for the parts. For all other clarinets, from the smallest down to the basset horn, the notation is always in treble clef (only the lowest notes of the basset horn, especially the *c*, were usually scored in bass clef by Mozart and his contemporaries, that is, as for the French horn, one fourth below the sound: and similarly for all saxophones from sopranino to contrabass).

The rarely used contrabass clarinet (in French, formerly: *clarinette pédale*) extends an octave below the bass clarinet. The first instrument of this kind was the *contrebasse guerrière* built by Dumas in 1808, which was not successful. The *bathyphon* invented in 1839 by Wilhelm Wieprecht, director of military music of the Prussian Guard Regiments, and made first by E. Skorra of Berlin and later also by C. Kruspe of Erfurt, became more widely known. Its tube of wood or metal is folded like a bassoon, the keys are arranged like

[1] Also Stravinsky in *The Rite of Spring*.

a keyboard; the compass of the C instrument is $E'-c'$. The bathyphon represents a surprisingly advanced product of German instrument making, and if it was employed for a short while only in Prussian military bands and never adopted by operatic or concert orchestras, the reason is probably to be found in the fact that in the low register the sound is too dull, while the very beautiful higher notes could be produced much more easily and agreeably on the bass clarinet which had been brought to perfection in that period. The awkward size of the mouthpiece also proved a hindrance to wider acceptance.

After Adolphe Sax's abortive attempts about 1840 to construct a technically and musically faultless contrabass clarinet, work in this field came to a standstill until it was taken up again 50 years later at the request of a composer, Isidore de Lara, by the Paris firm of Evette & Schaeffer. In 1889 it resulted in a B♭ contrabass clarinet which in the course of the following years underwent a number of alterations and probably inspired several other makers to build similar instruments.

At about the same time, the firm of Fontaine-Besson of Paris also produced an excellent contrabass clarinet which earned much praise from Saint-Saëns and which Vincent d'Indy specified in his opera *Fervaal* (Brussels, 1897). The instrument has a tube-length of $8\frac{3}{4}$ feet and consists of three wooden tubes of unequal length, connected by metal knee joints. Its written compass is $B-g''''$ (sounding $A''-f'$). The key mechanism is very similar to that of the soprano clarinet and it responds easily, so that any clarinettist is able to play the instrument without much previous practice.

In Germany, Wilhelm Heckel of Biebrich-am-Rhein concerned himself with the construction of a contrabass clarinet, and in 1897 produced an all-metal instrument reaching the sounding contra-D' (fig. 19). Its sound and response were excellent and it reaped particularly high praise from Felix Weingartner who employed the instrument in his opera *Orestes* (Leipzig, 1902).

In the present century, many firms in Europe and America have produced contrabass clarinets but most of them based on existing models. However an instrument with completely novel features was invented by Charles Houvenaghel and produced in 1930–31 by the Paris firm of G. Leblanc. The lowest note of this well thought-out instrument is the sounding sub-contra-$B''\flat$.

The *octo-bass clarinet* in B♭, also invented by Houvenaghel and built by Leblanc, goes one full octave lower still. This gigantic instrument was completed in the spring of 1939 and sent to the exhibition in New York. It is hardly likely to be of musical importance.

At its first use in d'Indy's *Fervaal*, the contrabass clarinet not only reinforced the bass but also played an important solo part. Weingartner in *Orestes* and Strauss in *Josephslegende* followed this example. In the latter work, the instrument is entrusted with a very significant solo passage, though in most performances this is taken over by the contrabassoon since so few orchestras possess a contrabass clarinet.

(Sounds one note lower)

Arnold Schönberg also specified a contrabass clarinet, e.g. in the first version of the five Orchestral Pieces, in the four *Lieder* Opus 22, and in his uncompleted opera *Moses and Aaron* (in A, although all existing instruments are in B♭). In his music drama *Penthesilea* (1927), Othmar Schoeck specifies 13 clarinets, among them one contrabass. Today, the instrument is occasionally used for special effects in light and film music. A concerto by the Dutch composer G. Landré for contrabass clarinet and orchestra may be mentioned as a curiosity.

Some wind bands favour the contrabass clarinet, e.g. the band of the Garde Républicaine. The full complement of the Harmonie de la Bouverie with 130 members comprises four contrabass clarinets, and Belgian military bands also use it. In 1939 it was introduced in German air force bands who employed instruments specifically constructed for them by Hüller of Schöneck in the Vogtland (fig. 22).

The contrabass clarinet sounds very soft and round, and is far more flexible than the contrabassoon. In contrast to the latter, it responds well even in the lowest *piano* notes (a general advantage of clarinets as compared with oboes and bassoons, and the reason, for instance, that the bassoon phrase in the first movement of Tchaikovsky's Sixth Symphony marked *pppppp* [sic] is normally played on a bass clarinet). However, it should be noted that air consumption for the lowest notes is greater than with the contra-bassoon, so that these notes cannot be produced as strongly and distinctly as on the latter. It was probably for this reason that higher-pitched contrabass clarinets have been built, e.g. Ernst Schmidt's contrabass clarinet in G (reaching the written low *d*) produced in the 1930s, and Selmer's contrabass clarinet in E♭, pitched a fifth lower than the bass clarinet.

Saxophone-like instruments, overblowing an octave, include the *Heckelphone clarinet* (fig. 23; markedly conical, wooden, sounding from *d* to *c″*), and the *Heckel-clarina* in B♭, constructed by W. Heckel prior to 1890. The latter closely resembles a soprano saxophone and has occasionally been used for the merry shepherd's dance in *Tristan* (compass, *a–c‴♯*, written one tone higher). The smaller *Heckel piccolo-clarina* in E♭ (compass, *d′–a‴*, written a minor third lower) also belongs in this group.

Among the conical instruments with single reed is the *Oktavin* invented in 1894 by J. Jehring and built by Oskar Adler of Mark-neukirchen. It is a cheap wooden instrument, slightly conical, and sounds from *a♭–f‴*; a bass oktavin has also been made.

The *tarogato* is a narrow-bore, conical wooden instrument with a single reed, oboe fingering and a compass of written *b♭–c‴*. It is made in three keys (B♭, E♭ and A♭), and is particularly popular in Hungary, being based on an old Hungarian national instrument of the same name which, however, had a double reed and thus belonged to the shawm family. (The ancestor of this instrument was a wooden signal trumpet; see also the article 'Tarogato' in *Grove's Dictionary of Music*, fifth edition.) In spite of the single reed, the tarogato has preserved its shawm-like sound of dark and piercing notes, not unlike the cor anglais. Johann Strauss is believed to have originally specified it for the solo in the overture of the *Zigeuner-baron*, now always executed on the oboe (see J. A. MacGillivray in A. Baines, *Musical Instruments*, Penguin Books, 1961). Mahler and

Hans Richter have employed it for the shepherd's air in *Tristan*.

The simple tarogato was modernised by W. Schunda of Budapest about 1900 and supplied with a modern key mechanism. The Budapest Conservatory made lessons available and Henrik Hiekisch wrote a tutor. The instrument has occasionally been used in Hungarian compositions: Antal Molnar wrote a *Kuruc Muzsika* for small orchestra and four tarogatos (1936), and his light opera *Gräfin Mariza* contains some beautiful solo passages for tarogato, which, however, are always played by the first clarinet.

The saxophone was invented by Adolphe Sax (1814–1894) and patented in France in 1846. It can be mentioned only briefly in these pages. Prior to Sax, about 1830, William Meikle built a conical wind instrument overblowing an octave and with a single reed (see Rendall, 'The Saxophone before Sax', *Mus.T.*, 1932). This 'alto fagotto' had the shape of a bassoon, except that it was distinctly more conical. Curt Sachs erroneously names H. Lazarus as the inventor and the time as about 1820, but Lazarus was not born until 1815. The name 'tenoroon' for this instrument is incorrect (tenoroon is another name for the quint-bassoon, an instrument of a higher pitch than the ordinary bassoon).

In contrast to the clarinet, the saxophone is markedly conical and consequently overblows an octave. For this reason, the fingering, based on Boehm's principles, is considerably easier and technically more perfect. All saxophones are of metal and have no finger-holes, only key-plates arranged according to acoustic principles (figs. 24, 25).

There are saxophones in eight sizes from the sopranino (in F or Eb) to the sub-contrabass (in Bb) but in practice, only the soprano saxophone in Bb, the alto in Eb, the tenor in Bb and the baritone in Eb are used. The sopranino saxophone and the bass saxophone (in Bb) are rare. No practical use is made of contrabass and sub-contrabass saxophones. The pitches C–F are occasionally prescribed instead of the more usual Bb–Eb. (Sax intended the C–F pitches for orchestras, the Bb–Eb pitches for military bands.)

The compass of present-day saxophones normally extends from (written) $b\flat$ to f'''; some instruments have an additional $f'''\sharp$ key (on alto and tenor), or a key for low *a* (on the baritone); earlier instruments extended from *b–e'''*♭. The saxophone has two 'automatic' octave keys, the first for the notes *d''* to *g''*♯; when the *g''* key is released, the second octave key opens and the first closes. Some makes have three octave keys, for easier response and tuning of *d''*.

The saxophone normally overblows only to the first partial, i.e. the octave. The notes from *d'''* to *f'''* (or *f'''*♯) consequently have to be produced by special keys on the upper joint whose fundamental tones are not used. Because of the wide bore, the higher harmonics do not respond very well, although with special fingerings (and special reeds) higher notes are possible. W. Rochow in his *Handbuch der Saxophon-Praxis* (Verlag Birnbaum, Berlin) indicates fingering up to *c''''*. Some players achieve *d''''* or even *f''''* but normally the instrument should not be taken higher than *f'''*.

A somewhat mellower tone may be achieved by means of a mute.

The sopranino saxophone in E♭ sounds a third higher than written; the soprano saxophone in B♭ one tone lower; the alto saxophone in E♭ one sixth lower, etc. Music for all saxophones is written in treble clef.

Mouthpiece and reed are wider than in the clarinet, the lays are much more open and the reeds lighter. In consequence, blowing demands much less pressure from the lips. Because of its quick response and relatively simple fingering, the saxophone is easier to learn than the clarinet, but a good tone quality—to which no great value is attached in light music—demands devoted study.

Many contemporary composers had nothing but praise for the newly invented instrument. Berlioz said in his *Modern Instrumentation*: 'These new voices given to the orchestra, possess most rare and precious qualities ..., especially in slow and soft pieces.' In *Le Journal de Débats* he wrote of the sound of the saxophone: 'In my opinion, its special qualities lie in the manifold beauty of expression—now solemn and serene, now passionate, sometimes dreamy or melancholy and then again dying away altogether ... no other instrument that I know of possesses this strange sound which stands in the borderland of silence.' Nevertheless, in the nineteenth century the saxophone was rarely used; it has been employed more frequently only in the twentieth century (during which it became well-known through jazz). Saxophones are chiefly used in dance, light and jazz music, as well as in larger wind bands; also occasionally in the more recent light operas.

In serious music the use of the saxophone is still an exception. According to Rendall, Berlioz wrote a *Chant Sacre* for six saxophones but never used it elsewhere. Among composers who used the saxophone in the orchestra are Kastner (*Le Dernier Roi de Juda*, 1844) Meyerbeer, Thomas (*Hamlet, Françoise da Rimini*) Massenet (*Hérodiade, Werther*), Saint-Saëns (*Jeunesse d'Hercule*), Bizet (*L'Arlèsienne*, with a famous solo for alto saxophone in the first Suite), d'Indy (*Fervaal*), Puccini (*Turandot*), R. Strauss (*Symphonia Domestica*, ad libitum soprano in C, alto in F, baritone in F and bass in C), Ravel (*Bolero*, with solos for tenor and sopranino saxophones; and in his orchestration of Mussorgsky's *Pictures from an Exhibition*), Hindemith (*Cardillac, Neues vom Tage*), Stravinsky, Bartók, Honegger (*Johanna*), Berg (Violin Concerto, *Lulu*), Henze (*Antigone, Prinz von Homburg*), Krenek (*Johnny spielt auf*).

Among those who wrote concert pieces for saxophone and orchestra are Debussy (*Rhapsody*, 1904, also playable with piano), d'Indy (*Choral varié*, 1903), Ibert (Concertino), E. Koch, G. Raphael, Zender, K. G. Breuer (*Atonalyse II*), J. Jongen (*Méditation*), H. Badings (Alto Saxophone Concerto, 1915), A. Glazunov (Concerto, 1934), Páleniček.

Chamber music with saxophone has been composed by, amongst others, Paul Hindemith (Sonata for alto horn in E♭ or alto saxophone, Trio for viola, heckelphone or tenor saxophone and piano), Günther Raphael (Sonata and Recitative for alto saxophone and piano, Divertimento for alto saxophone and cello), M. Delannoy (Rhapsody for trumpet, alto saxophone, cello and piano), Anton Webern (Quartet Opus 22 for clarinet, tenor saxophone, violin and piano), A. Ebel (two Intermezzi for saxophone and cello), H. C. Görner (Concertino for two saxophones and piano).

Bozza, Eisenmann, Engelmann, Dressel, Ibert, Krol, Martin, Martelli, Pepping, Tscherepnin, Tomasi, Leinert (Sonata, 1952), W. Girnatis (Sonatina) and Françaix (5 Dances) have written music for saxophone and piano.

Saxophone quartets (soprano, alto, tenor and baritone) have a beautiful tone quality; this chamber music instrumentation made its name particularly in France and chiefly through the Marcel Mule Quartet of the Paris Conservatoire, founded in 1928. Among the composers for quartet are Pierné, J. François, Françaix, Bozza, Glazunov and others.

SHORT BIOGRAPHIES OF SOME
EMINENT CLARINETTISTS

JOHANN CHRISTOPH DENNER

Johann Christoph Denner was born in Leipzig on 13 August 1655, the son of a Nuremberg 'hunting-horn turner' (*Jägerhorndreher*), Heinrich Denner. When he was eight years old, his parents moved back to Nuremberg and there he 'assiduously' learnt from his father the trade of 'turning horn and decoy calls'[1] (Doppelmayr). Becoming one of the best instrument-makers of his time, he not only built excellent and generally popular recorders, oboes and bassoons but also variously improved the woodwind instruments, and finally evolved the clarinet from the earlier chalumeau.[2] Very probably Denner was a practising musician as well as a maker, for the entry in the register of deaths speaks of him as *Musicus und Flöttenmacher*, and Doppelmayr records that 'he was most proficient in music, although he never had a teacher'. Denner died on 20 April 1707, and left his business to his two sons, Jacob (d. 1735) and Matthäus (d. 1740) who 'increased their father's fame by continuing the skilful manufacture of these instruments and their artistic use' (Doppelmayr). Schubart, giving a somewhat exaggerated account of their flourishing trade, says that they sold instruments by the crateful all over Europe and brought home 'a profit of thousands' from their travels. 'Their profit was so enormous that they were able to buy large estates and still have thousands left.' However, contemporary documents give no indication of great fortunes. Both brothers died as musicians and instrument-makers in Nuremberg.

---

[1] (*Wildruff- und Horn-Drehen*) small instruments used by hunters to imitate the calls of game.

[2] It is somewhat misleading to speak of the 'invention' of the clarinet, and the accounts given by G. R. Kruse in his libretto for the opera *Der Klarinettenmacher* (music by F. Weigmann; first performance in Bamberg, 1913), and by the sources he used, are wholly fictitious.

ANTON STADLER

Anton Stadler and his brother lived in the Vienna of Mozart and were celebrated clarinettists. The brothers are believed to have been employed first by Prince Gallitzin. In 1783 they joined the Imperial *Harmoniemusik*, consisting of eight wind players, and in 1787 the court orchestra, which had not previously employed a clarinettist. Although Anton began as a second player and only later took his brother's place as first clarinettist, he was far better known. He died in Vienna on 15 June 1812 at the age of 59, having retired as early as 1799. Johann Stadler died in 1804 at the age of 48.

In musical history Anton Stadler has the dishonourable reputation of having exploited his friendship with Mozart. While the composer wrote many a brilliant score for him, occasionally helped him when he was in financial straits, and, it must be admitted, often made him the butt of some good-natured, friendly teasing,[1] Stadler betrayed him shamelessly. He figures in the probate proceedings after Mozart's death as a bad debtor to the tune of 500 florins.

Stadler made his name not only as a clarinettist but also as an improver of the clarinet and a composer. Some of his short works are still to be found in certain libraries and prove his skill as a composer for various fashionable instruments, as well as for the basset horn and the clarinet.

IVAN MÜLLER

Ivan (or Iwan) Müller was born on 3 December 1786, in Reval, the son of German parents. Nothing definite is known about his youth and training, but when he went to Paris in 1809 to publicise his improved clarinet, he was already known in Germany as a successful clarinet virtuoso. An unfavourable verdict of the academy caused the instrument-making business he had set up with financial backing from the banker Petit, to collapse, and he left Paris in 1820 to go to Russia. Three years later he returned to Germany where he found employment first in Kassel (1825) and later in Berlin. In 1826 he travelled to Switzerland and subsequently to England. He returned to Paris after the July Revolution. He died as court musician to the Prince of Schaumberg-Lippe on 4 February 1854, in Bückeburg, where his grave may be seen in the Jetenburg cemetery.

At the height of his artistic career, Ivan Müller was renowned for the beautiful tone, the graceful and elegant phrasing and the fiery manner of his performances (Fétis). His clarinet tutor and concerts were very popular in his lifetime but are now almost completely forgotten.

[1] Mozart gave his friend the nickname *Notschibikitschi*, composed of two typical Viennese expressions. A *Notschibi* is a poor wretch or a miser, and *Kitschibi* is a name given to people who talk a lot of nonsense.

HYACINTHE ELEONORE KLOSÉ

Hyacinthe Eleonore Klosé was born on 11 October 1808, on the Isle of Corfu. He came to France at an early age and there joined a military band as a clarinettist. He perfected his art under the instruction of the famous clarinettist Frédéric Berr[1] and, on the death of his master, took his place as professor at the Paris Conservatoire. He retired in 1868 and died in Paris on 29 August 1880.

Although Klosé was enormously successful in Paris as a soloist and his beautiful tone and exemplary phrasing earned the highest praise of the critics, he very rarely travelled and probably never crossed the frontiers of his country. He devoted all his time to teaching numerous pupils and the work connected with that task. He wrote an excellent clarinet tutor which is still in use, many études and solo pieces. For the newly created saxophone he wrote three tutors, adapted to the different pitches of the instrument, and in his capacity as musical director of a division of the National Guard, he composed some works for military band.

Klosé earned for himself a lasting place in musical history by his application of Boehm's ring-key system to the clarinet and thus the construction of an instrument which—almost unchanged—to this day satisfies the demands of professional musicians of many countries, and has also given important stimuli to the 'German' clarinet system.

JOHANN SIMON HERMSTEDT

Johann Simon Hermstedt was born on 29 December 1778, in Langensalza, the son of an army musician, and up to the age of 16 was educated in a school for the sons of soldiers, at Annaberg. Having spent five years as an apprentice in various municipal bands, he enlisted in 1799 as first clarinettist in his father's regiment. While the regiment was temporarily stationed in Dresden, he perfected his musical knowledge. When on one occasion the Prince of Sondershausen heard the band, he was so impressed with its performance that he engaged the young Hermstedt and commissioned him to found a similar *Harmoniemusik*.[2] In 1802 Hermstedt received a firm appointment and in 1809 was promoted to the post of the Prince's chamber musician, a year later to musical director, and in 1824 to Kapellmeister. The *Harmoniemusik* was dissolved when the court orchestra was founded

---

[1] Frédéric Berr was born in 1794 in Mannheim. He played in the bands of various French regiments and later, as first clarinettist, in the Royal Orchestra in the Théâtre Italien in Paris. In 1831 he was appointed to the professorship at the Paris Conservatoire, and in 1836 became director of the new school of military music. He died in Paris in 1838.

[2] Two oboes, two clarinets, two bassoons, two trumpets, two horns, in addition to a bass horn (bassoon-shaped instrument with cup mouthpiece and keys) and a trombone.

in 1835, and Hermstedt was given the title of court Kapellmeister and thus entrusted with the leadership of the orchestra, a post which he filled until his retirement in 1839. Hermstedt died on 10 August 1846, from a throat disease caused, it was believed, by his untiring work on the clarinet.

Hermstedt's fame is chiefly due to his fingering technique whose outstanding excellence was enthusiastically acclaimed by the critics, while the manner of his musical performance was not always the subject of unanimous praise. C. M. von Weber wrote: 'Twice Hermstedt played very beautifully. A thick, almost stuffy tone. Surmounts tremendous difficulties but not always pleasingly, sometimes altogether against the nature of the instrument. Also agreeable execution. Uses many violin strokes which can be quite effective but lacks Baermann's uniform quality of tone from high to low and heavenly tastefulness of execution.' Even Spohr was not invariably pleased with his clarinettist. Although he once called him 'the most excellent of living clarinet virtuosi', in his autobiography he remarks: 'However, I found, and several other musicians were of the same opinion, that Hermstedt does not develop his taste to the same extent, though he continues to improve his technique. His performance is full of mannerisms, verging on caricature.' It appears that Hermstedt in later years—perhaps under Weber's influence?—achieved the kind of execution for which Baermann was famous, so that some critics gave him higher praise even than his model and competitor.

Goethe was extremely pleased with his playing. Hermstedt met Weber in 1815 and the composer was to write a clarinet concerto for him (left unfinished).

Hermstedt travelled extensively in Germany and Austria and also in Holland. Although some critics of musical journals accused him of being superficial in his musical performance, he was a great success wherever he went. Hermstedt did not compose very much. His attempts to improve the clarinet have already been mentioned.

THOMAS LINDSAY WILLMAN

Thomas Lindsay Willman (about 1774-1840) was the most renowned British clarinet virtuoso of his time because of his beautiful, singing tone. Willman still played with the reed upwards, which favours a tone resembling the human voice. He liked to share the platform with female singers (Catalani, Sontag, Malibran, Salmon) and played a 13-keyed instrument for which he wrote an excellent tutor in 1825.

In 1838 he played in the first London performance of Mozart's Clarinet Concerto which was not widely known at that time. The critics regarded it as spurious, 'a product of the laboratory of André'.

It is believed that Willman first played in the East India Company's

36 Johann Sobeck (1831–1914)

37 Richard Mühlfeld
(1856–1907)

38 Robert Stark
(1847–1922)

39 Oskar Oehler (1858–1936)

Volunteer Band under C. Eley. Later he became bandmaster in the Coldstream Guards (until 1825). He succeeded W. Mahon in the Philharmonic and operatic orchestra. He also played the basset horn.

HEINRICH BAERMANN

Heinrich Baermann was born on 14 February 1784, in Potsdam, and received his first musical instruction at the bandsman's school of the Potsdam military orphanage. He was a pupil of the renowned clarinettist Beer. In 1798 he joined the band of the Second Guard Regiment and thus came to the attention of Prince Louis Ferdinand who frequently commanded his attendance at musical entertainments and arranged for his further instruction by Franz Tausch. In the war of 1806 Baermann was taken prisoner by the French at Jena but escaped and went to Munich in search of employment with a letter of recommendation from Crown Prince Ludwig of Bavaria. After a recital at a court concert, he was engaged as first clarinettist in the court orchestra. He was succeeded in this post by his son Carl who had already worked for some years with his father in the orchestra. Baermann died in Munich on 11 June 1847.

Baermann undertook several concert tours throughout almost the whole of Europe. In 1808 he was in Switzerland and the South of France, and in 1811 he met C. M. von Weber with whom he visited Gotha, Weimar, Dresden, Prague and Berlin. In 1813 he was in Vienna and two years later he travelled in Italy where he met with tumultuous applause. In the winter of 1817–18 he gave concerts with Angelica Catalani[1] in Paris. In 1819 he spent six months in London at the invitation of the Philharmonic Society, and two years later he was planning a visit to Russia but broke his journey in Berlin and went, instead, to Vienna where he remained and gave concerts for four months. His Russian tour was postponed until 1822 when he went to St Petersburg, via Switzerland, Strasbourg, Frankfurt, Kassel, Hamburg and Riga. He twice appeared at court and after an absence of 16 months returned to Munich via Moscow, Warsaw, Breslau and Prague. In 1827 he undertook a shorter journey to Copenhagen. In order to introduce his son to the musical world as clarinettist and basset horn player, he took him on a return visit to St Petersburg in 1832, from where father and son did not return until 1834. Baermann's second visit to Paris in 1839 served the same purpose. On that occasion, the critics called him the 'Rubini'[2] of the clarinet. His last journey in 1843 is said to have been to Holland.

[1] Famous singer, 1780–1849. Baermann shared the platform with her on several later occasions.
[2] Giovanni Battiste Rubini, a famous tenor, 1795–1854. Appeared with enormous success in 1825–26 in the Paris Théâtre Italien.

Baermann's fame as a clarinettist was founded not so much on his finger-technique, which was the case with Hermstedt, as on the 'perfect equality of tone from high to low and the heavenly tastefulness of execution'. No doubt his technical skill was considerable but it did not dominate his performance. The critics mentioned chiefly 'his pleasing and singing tone' and he was venerated as a 'truly profound artist' who 'resisted every temptation to go crooked ways or indulge in fashionable nonsense'. But C. M. von Weber paid the highest tribute to 'his dear friend' when he spoke of him in a letter as 'a truly great artist and a wonderful person'. H. J. Baermann's brother, Carl Baermann, was a well-known bassoonist in the service of the King of Prussia. He also travelled extensively and wrote musical works. He died on the day of his retirement, 31 March 1842, in Berlin.

CARL BAERMANN

Carl Baermann, son of H. J. Baermann and Helene Harlas, a primadonna at the court theatre, was born in Munich on 24 October 1811. He began to take clarinet lessons in early childhood and at the age of 14 was allowed to play in the court orchestra where three years later he was employed as '*élève*' (pupil) and in 1832 as court musician. Carl Baermann remained in this post until his retirement in 1880 after 50 years service, but continued to work for two further years as teacher at the school of music. He died on 23 March 1885.

Carl Baermann's father had introduced his son to the musical world in the course of the two grand tours mentioned above. Subsequently he travelled frequently, in Germany, Austria and Hungary, though owing to the unfavourable circumstances of the time his success never matched that of his father. But recognition was not lacking and he received many diplomas, medals and orders, and was appointed professor at the Royal School of Music in Munich.

Carl Baermann's compositions met with great success. Though few of his many concertos and chamber music works are known today, his clarinet tutor remains the most important work in the whole range of study literature for the clarinet. He also earned some renown for his improvements of the instrument.

His son Karl (1839–1913) was one of Franz Liszt's outstanding pupils. He worked for many years at the Munich Academy of Music until he emigrated to America.

RICHARD MÜHLFELD

Richard Mühlfeld was born on 28 February 1856, the fourth child of *Stadtmusikus* Leonhard Mühlfeld in Bad Salzungen (Thuringia). At the early age of 17 he joined the Meiningen court orchestra as violinist. He had learnt the elements of clarinet playing in childhood and now continued to study on his own to such good purpose that after his military service he was able, in 1879, to take on the responsible post of first clarinettist in the Meiningen court orchestra and to satisfy even the critical Hans von Bülow. With the backing of his friend Brahms he achieved European fame as a chamber music player. In his turn, he made Brahms' works widely known on his many concert tours through Germany, Austria, Hungary, Denmark, Britain, Holland, Belgium, France and Switzerland.

On some of these tours, he was accompanied by Brahms and the famous violinist Joseph Joachim. In view of the sweet tone of his instrument, Brahms called him 'Miss Clarinet'. From 1884–1896 Mühlfeld was solo clarinettist in the Bayreuth Festival Orchestra.

In 1888 Mühlfeld took on the directorship of the stage and entr'acte orchestra at the Meiningen court theatre and three years later was appointed musical director to the Duke of Meiningen. He died of a cerebral haemorrhage on 1 June 1907.

Mühlfeld was not a virtuoso of the old school which sought to dazzle the audience with a supreme fingering technique and superficial effects; his strength lay in a profoundly musical expression. It was this that attracted Brahms to Mühlfeld whom he called the 'nightingale of the orchestra'. In a letter to Clara Schumann, Brahms said: 'It is impossible to play the clarinet more beautifully than Herr Mühlfeld here.'

ROBERT STARK

Robert Stark was born on 19 September 1847, in Klingenthal (Saxony), the son of an instrument-maker. He took his first clarinet lessons at the early age of five. Later he learnt to play various brass instruments as well and before he had reached the age of 14, he joined a Saxon Infantry Regiment as bugler. While in the army, he continued to work untiringly at his musical education, and in the winter of 1868–69 completed his studies at the Dresden Conservatory. In 1871 Stark joined the Chemnitz orchestra under Müller-Berghaus who engaged him as a solo clarinettist in Wiesbaden two years later. In 1881 he was called to a teaching post for clarinet, wind ensemble and piano to the Würzburg school of music. Here he wrote his great study works for the clarinet and endeavoured to improve the instrument. Stark received the title of 'Royal Professor' in 1904 and retired in 1919. He died in Würzburg on 29 October 1922.

Regrettably, Stark did not achieve the fame as virtuoso to which, perhaps, he was entitled. He devoted his entire energy to his pupils and the composition of his magnificent study works. Today, his great tutor and his études are known and used all over the world. As a composer, Stark became known for his concertos and concert pieces for the clarinet and other instruments, through his *Lieder*, choral works, chamber music, and orchestral works.

OSKAR OEHLER

Oskar Oehler was born on 2 February 1858, at Annaberg (Erz Mountains), and at the age of 15 was apprenticed to an organ builder. Here he acquired an elementary knowledge of building and playing the clarinet. After a spell with the municipal orchestra in Weide, he joined the Halle theatre orchestra, and subsequently Müller-Berghaus called him to Nice. In 1881 he returned to Germany to take up an appointment with the famous Laube Orchestra in Hamburg. In the following year he took part in a London performance of the *Ring* under Anton Seidl. He was a co-founder of the Berlin Philharmonic Orchestra and remained a member until 1888.

On his concert tours, Oehler made contact with other distinguished clarinettists to ask their advice for his studies on the construction of instruments, mouthpieces and reeds. He was fortunate enough to meet players who had been closely associated with the great era of wind instrument virtuosi. In Munich he collaborated with Carl Baermann, in Kassel with the clarinettist A. Neff who had played with Hermstedt under Spohr. Thus, Oehler collected the most important experiences of many outstanding clarinettists of several generations.

While with the Berlin Philharmonic, Oehler had been concerned with the construction of mouthpieces and attempts to improve the clarinet, and he finally decided to terminate his career as a musician and devote himself entirely to instrument-making. In 1887 he started a workshop in the Alvenslebenstrasse and three years later moved to Katzlerstrasse where, with astonishing energy, he served German clarinettists until his death on 1 October 1936.

BIBLIOGRAPHY

Readers who desire further information beyond the scope of this book are advised to consult F. G. Rendall's work *The Clarinet* which contains details about British circumstances which had to be omitted from this book, as well as a list of the most important English publications. See also Rendall's article 'Clarinet' in *Grove's Dictionary of Music* (fifth edition).

Special mention should be made of an excellent article 'Klarinette' in *Die Musik in Geschichte und Gegenwart*, edited by F. Blume, Kassel–Basel–New York, vol. 7, 1958. The article is in three parts, with a list of the most important literature in each case: Acoustics (by Professor W. Stauder); Non-European and Antique Clarinet Instruments (by Professor H. Hickmann); European Clarinets (by Professor H. Becker, who has recently published several outstanding works about the clarinet, see list below).

Altenburg, J. E., *Versuch einer Anleitung zur heroisch-musikalischen Trompeter- und Pauker-Kunst*, Halle 1795

Altenburg, W., *Die Klarinette*, Heilbronn 1904

Backofen, J. G. H., *Anweisung zur Clarinette*, 1803

Baines, A., *Woodwind Instruments and their History*, London 1957

Becker, H., 'Zur Geschichte der Klarinette im 18. Jahrh.', *Die Musikforschung*, VIII, 1955, pp. 271–92; foreword to *Klar.-Duette aus der Frühzeit des Instrumentes*, Wiesbaden 1954; foreword to *Klar.-Konzerte des 18. Jahrh.*, Erbe deutscher Musik, Vol. 41, Wiesbaden 1957; *Studien zur Geschichte der Rohrblattinstrumente* (Habil.-Schr. Hamburg 1961)

Boese, H., 'Die Klarinette als Soloinstrument in der Musik der Mannheimer Schule', *Phil. Diss. Berlin* 1940

Brenet, M., 'Rameau, Gossec et les clarinettes', *Le Guide musicale*, Paris and Brussels 1903

Burbure, L. de, *Les oeuvres des anciens musiciens belges*, Brussels 1882

Chatwin, R. B., 'Handel and the Clarinet', *Galpin Society Journal*, 1950

Cucuel, G., 'La question des clarinettes dans l'instrumentation du XVIIIe siècle', *Zeitschrift der Internat. Musikgesellschaft XII*, 1910–11, p. 280 ff.

Diderot and d'Alembert, *Encyclopédie*.

Dittersdorf, K. D. von, *Lebensbeschreibung nach dem Erstdruck*, ed. B. Loets, Leipzig 1940

Doppelmayr, J. G., *Nachrichten von den Nürnberger Mathematicis und Künstlern*, 1730

Eisel, J. Ph., *Musicus autodidactus*, Erfurt 1738

Elsenaar, E., *De clarinet*, Hilversum 1929

Engel, H., 'Das Instrumentalkonzert' in *Kretzschmars Führer durch den Konzertsaal*, vol. 3, Leipzig 1932

Fétis, F. J., *Bibliographie universelle des musiciens* . . . , Brussels 1837–44

Fröhlich, J., *Systematischer Unterricht in den vorzüglichsten Orchesterinstrumenten*, 1829

Gabucci, A., *Origine e storia del Clarinetto*, Milan 1937

Gerber, E. L., *Historisch-biographisches Lexicon*, Leipzig 1790–92; *Neues historisch-biographisches Lexicon*, Leipzig 1812–14

Gevaert, F. A., *Neue Instrumenten-Lehre*, H. Riemann, Leipzig 1887

Gollmick, C., 'Ein Wort über die Verbesserung der Klarinette', *Allgemeine musikalische Zeitung*, 1845

Gradenwitz, P., 'The Beginnings of Clarinet Literature', *Music and Letters*, April 1947

Hanslick, E., *Geschichte des Concertwesens in Wien*, Vienna 1869–71; *Concerte, Componisten und Virtuosen der letzten 15 Jahre*, Berlin 1886

Hiller, J. A., *Wöchentliche Nachrichten* . . . , 1769, 1777

Kappey, J. A., *Military Music*, London 1894

Karstädt, G., Article 'Saxinstrumente' in *MGG*

Klosé, H., *Méthode de clarinette*, Paris 1843

Kolneder, W., 'Die Klarinette bei Vivaldi', *Die Musikforschung*, 1951, pp. 185–91, and 1955, pp. 209–11

Komorzynsky, E. von, *Mozarts Kunst der Instrumentation*, Stuttgart 1906

Kool, J., *Das Saxophon*, Leipzig 1931

Kroll, O., 'Das Chalumeau', *Zeitschrift für Musikwissenschaft*, xv, 1932, p. 374 ff.

Kunitz, H., *Die Instrumentation*, vol. IV 'Klarinette', Leipzig 1957

Laborde, J. B. de, *Essai sur la musique* . . . , vol. I, Paris 1780

Langwill, G., *An Index of Musical Wind-Instrument Makers*, Edinburgh 1960

Laurencie, L. de la, 'Rameau et les clarinettes', *Sammelbände der Internat. Musikgesellschaft*, 1913

Mahillon, V. C., *Catalogue du Musée instrumental du conservatoire*, Brussels 1909 ff.

Majer, J. F. B. C., *Museum musicum*, Nürnberg 1732 (facsimile, Kassel 1954); *Neu eröffneter Music-Saal*, 1741

Mattheson, J., *Das neu-eröffnete Orchester*, 1713

Menke, W., *Das Vokalwerk G. Ph. Telemanns*, Kassel 1942

Mixa, F., 'Die Klarinette bei Mozart', *Phil. Diss. Wien* 1929

Müller, I., *Anweisung zu der neuen Clarinette und der Clarinette-Alto*, Leipzig 1825

Oppermann, K., *Repertory of Clarinet*, New York 1960

Paumgartner, B., *Mozart*, Berlin 1927; 'Die Instrumentation Mozarts', *Das Orchester*, 1929

Pierre, C., *Les facteurs d'instrument de musique*, Paris 1893; *La facture instrumentale*, Paris 1890

Pincherle, M., *Antonio Vivaldi et la musique instrumentale*, Paris 1948

Pohl, C. F, *Haydn*, vol. II, Leipzig 1882

Pontécoulant, A. de, *Organographie*, vol. II, Paris 1861

Prod'homme, J. G., 'Notes d'archives concernant l'emploi des clarinettes en 1763', *Bulletin S. F. de M.*, 1919

Reich, W., 'Bemerkungen zu Mozarts Klarinettenkonzert', *Zeitschrift für Musikwissenschaft*, xv, 1933, p. 276 f.

Rendall, F. G., *The Clarinet*, London 1954, 2nd rev. ed., London 1957; Article 'Clarinet' in *Grove's Dictionary of Music* . . . , 5th ed. 1954; 'The Saxophone before Sax', *Mus. T.*, December 1932; 'A Short Account of the Clarinet in England', *P.M.A.*, LXVIII, 1942

Riemann, H., *Musiklexikon*, 1922; new ed. 1959

Sachs, C., *Reallexikon der Musikinstrumente*, Berlin 1913; *Handbuch der Musikinstrumentenkunde*, Leipzig 1920

Schiedermair, L., 'Die Oper an den badischen Höfen', *Sammelbände der Internationalen Musikgesellschaft*, XIV, 1912, p. 3 ff.

Schilling, G., *Universal-Lexikon der Tonkunst*, Stuttgart 1835–42

Schletterer, H. M., *Verzeichnis der Werke von L. Spohr*, Leipzig 1881; *Vorrede zu Spohrs III. Klar.-Konzert*

Schneider, W., *Historisch-technische Beschreibung der musicalischen Instrumente*, 1834

Schreiber, O., 'Orchester und Orchesterpraxis in Deutschland zwischen 1780 und 1850', *Phil. Diss. Berlin* 1938

Schubart, D., *Ideen zu einer Ästhetik der Tonkunst*, Vienna 1806

Spohr, L., *Selbstbiographie*, Kassel and Göttingen 1861

Tenschert, R., 'Fragment eines Klar.-Quintetts von W. A. Mozart', *Zeitschrift für Musikwissenschaft*, XIII, 1930/31, p. 218 ff.

Walther, J. G., *Musicalisches Lexicon* . . . , 1732 (facsimile, Kassel 1953)

Weber, M. M. von., *Carl Maria von Weber*, Leipzig 1864–1866

Weigel, J. Chr., *Musicalisches Theatrum*, Nürnberg *c.* 1740 (facsimile, Kassel 1959)

Whewell, M., 'Mozart's Bassethorn Trios', *Mus. T.*, January 1962

Zinzendorf, Graf, unprinted diary in the Staatsarchiv, Vienna

The following list represents only a selection from the large number of chamber music and concert compositions for the clarinet, mainly works which are in print at present or, at least, were available a short time ago. A large number of compositions long since out of print, which exist today only in a few copies or in manuscript form in libraries or private ownership, had to be omitted so as not to enlarge the list unduly. Therefore, obviously contemporary literature dominates.

The list is divided into sections according to instrumentation and within the sections composers are listed alphabetically.

Example: Honegger, A., Rhapsodie (2 Fl, Cl, P), 1917, *Senart 1923, Salabert.* i.e. Rhapsody by A. Honegger for 2 flutes, clarinet and piano (see list of abbreviations), composed in 1917, first published by Senart in 1923, and also by Salabert.

The title of a composition is omitted where it coincides with the title of the particular section in which it occurs (e.g. Trio, Wind Quintet, Clarinet Concerto, etc.). An indication of the instrumentation is omitted where it is obvious (e.g. Duets for Clarinet and Violin). As a rule, where a piece has been published by several firms, not all the publishers are listed.

CONTENTS

ABBREVIATIONS: INSTRUMENTS

A-Cl	A Clarinet	E♭-Cl	E ♭ Clarinet
Alt-Cl	Alto Clarinet	Fag	Bassoon
Alt-Fl	Alto Flute	Fl	Flute
A-Sax	Alto Saxophone	Ob	Oboe
Bass-Tr	Bass Trumpet	P	Pianoforte
Bar-Sax	Baritone Saxophone	Sax	Saxophone
Batt	Percussion (Batteria)	Tamb. picc.	Side drum
B♭-Cl	B ♭ Clarinet	Ten-Sax	Tenor Saxophone
Bcl	Bass Clarinet	Tr	Trumpet
Bh	Basset-horn	Trbne	Trombone
Cb	Double bass	V	Violin
Cfg	Contrabassoon	Va	Viola
CIngl	Cor anglais	Vc	Violoncello
Cl	Clarinet	Vibr	Vibraphone
Cor	French horn	Xyl	Xylophone
D-Cl	D Clarinet		

ABBREVIATIONS: PUBLISHERS

AMP	Associated Music Publishers Inc., New York
Bä	Bärenreiter
B & B	Bote & Bock
Br & H	Breitkopf & Härtel
By & H	Boosey & Hawkes
Cebedem	Centre Belge de Documentation Musicale
DFM	Dan Fog Musikforlag, Copenhagen
Donemus	Documentatie in Nederland van Muziek
EMB	Editio Musica Budapest
MAB	Musica Antiqua Bohemica
OUP	Oxford University Press
PMK	Polnischer Musikverlag Krakow
PSPH	Polish State Publishing House, Warsaw
Ric	Ricordi
SD	Stichting Donemus
SM	Skandinavisk Musikforlag, Copenhagen
SMC	Southern Music Comp.
SNKLHU	Státní Nakladetelstvi Krasne Literatury, Hudby A Uméni, Prague
SPAM	Society for the Publishing of American Music
UE	Universal Edition

A   Clarinet and Orchestra

1 *Concertos and concert pieces for clarinet and orchestra*

Amellier, A., Cantilène, *Leduc 1952*
Arnold, Malcolm, (string orchestra) *Lengnick 1951, Mills*
Bentzon, J., Kammerkoncert No. 3, op. 39, 1943, *DFM*
Berezovsky, N. T., op. 28, *By & H 1941*
Bernaud, Lyrisches Konzert, *Leduc*
Bertocini, M., Capriccio, 1953, *Ric*
Bialas, G., *Bä*
di Biase, E., Fantasia, 1942, Heugel, *Mercury 1953*
Blasius, M. F., Concerto II, *McGinnis & Marx*
Bloch, W., *Doblinger*
Bonneau, Suite, *Leduc*
Bonsel, A., *Donemus 1950*
Bozza, E., *Leduc 1952*
Breuer, K. G., Atonalyse I für Cl und Streicher, *Sikorski*
Bruns, V., Konzert op. 26, *Hofmeister*
Brusselmans, M., Recitativo e Aria, *Salabert 1930*
Busoni, F., Concertino op. 48, *Br & H 1920*
Cahuzac, L., Variations, *Leduc*
Camargo Guarnieri, M., Chôro, 1948, *Ric*
Casanova, A., Ballade op. 9, 1955, *Ric*
Cooke, A., *Novello*
Copland, A., *By & H 1952*
Crusell, B., op. 5 F-minor, *Sikorski*
Debussy, C., Première Rhapsodie, *Durand 1910*
Dresden, S., Symphonietta, *de Wolfe*
Felix, V., Phantasie op. 9, *Artia, Prague*
Fibich, Z., Idylle, *Bä*
Finzi, G., *By & H 1951*
Gagnebin, Andante et Allegro, *Leduc*
Hauck, F., Concertino, *Gerig*
Heider, W., Strophen, *Peters*
Hindemith, P., (A-Cl), *Schoot 1950*
Hlobil, E., Rhapsodie op. 51, *Artia, Prague*
Hoddinott, A., Konzert op. 3, *OUP 1950*
Horowitz, J., Concertante, *Chester 1952*
Jongen, J., Concertino op. 132, *Gervan, Brussels 1947*
Keys, I., *Novello*
Klebe, G., op. 23 Raskolnikows Traum, *B & B*
Klein, R. R., Fantasie für Cl und Streicher, *Gerig*
Koppel, H. D., (A-Cl) op. 35, 1941, *SM*

Kramář, Fr. op. 36, *André, MAB*
Krenek, E., Suite, *Bä*
Kubín, R., *Kudelík 1946*
Kubizek, A., op. 9, *Doblinger*
Landré, G., 4 Miniaturen, *Donemus*
Lutosławski, W., Tänzerische Praeludien, *PMK*
Macdonald, M., Cuban Rondo, 1961, *Ric*
Meulemans, A., Sonata Concertante, 1948, *Cebedem*
Milhaud, D., *Elkan-Vogel 1942*
Mirouze, M., Humoresque, *Leduc*
Molter, J. M., 4 Konzerte (D-Cl), *c.* 1740 (with String Orchestra and
    Cembalo), *Br & H 1957*
Mozart, W. A., A major (A-Cl) K 622, *André 1802*, four other editions
    Kadenz von Busoni, *Br & H 1922*, Kadenz von Ibert, *Leduc*
Nielsen, C., (A-Cl) op. 57, *Kistner 1931, DFM 1950*
Ollone, Max d', Fantasie Orientale, *Evette*
Pierné, G., Canzonetta, *Leduc*
Pitt, P., Concertino op. 22, *Boosey 1898*
Pokorny, F. X., 2 Konzerte, *c.* 1770, *Br & H 1957*
Quinet, M., Ballade, 1961, *Cebedem*
Rasse, F., La Dryade, 1943, *Gervan, Brussels*
Rawsthorne, A., *OUP 1936*
Reissiger, C. G., Concertino op. 63, *Schmidt* (2me Fantasie op. 180,
    Hofmeister) (Adagio und Rondo alla Polacca, *Hofmeister 1861*)
Reiter, A., *Doblinger*
Rimsky-Korsakov, N., *Omega 1949, Anglo-Soviet*
Riotte, Ph. J., *Sikorski*
Rossini, G., Introduktion, Thema und Variationen, *Sikorski*
Roussel, A., Aria, *Leduc*
Rueff, J., Concertino op. 15, *Leduc*
Schibler, A., Concerto op. 49, *Peters*
Schneider, G. A., Sinfonie concertante F-Dur, *B & B*
Seiber, M., Concertino, *Schott 1952, McGinnis & Marx*
Shaw, A., Concerto for Clarinet, *Mills*
Siegmeister, E., 1957, *Templeton*
Sikorski, K., *PMK*
Sosen, O. E. v., Arioso, *Peters*
Spohr, L., Nr. 1 op. 26, *Peters 1922*
  Nr. 2 op. 57, *Peters 1922*
  Nr. 3, *Br & H 1885*
  Nr. 4, *Br & H 1885*
  Fantasie und Variationen op. 81, *C. F. Schmidt*
  Thema und Var. aus 'Alruna', *C. F. Schmidt*

Stamitz, J., *Musicofot, Tel Aviv, Leeds*
Stamitz, K., Konzert E♭-Dur, *Sikorski*
  Konzert B-Dur Nr. 10, *Sikorski*
  Konzert E♭-Dur, 'Darmstädter', *Hofmeister*
Strategier, H., Concertino, *Donemus 1950*
Stravinsky, I., Ebony Concerto for Clarinet and Jazz Band, *Charling*
Szervánszky, E., Serenade, *EMB*
Tomasi, H., Konzert, *Leduc 1957*
  Introduction et Danse, *Leduc*
Veale, J., *OUP*
Weber, C. M., Concertino op. 26, *Br & H, Schmidt*
  1. Konzert op. 73 F-moll, *Br & H*
  2. Konzert op. 74 E♭-Dur, *Br & H*
Weiner, L., Ballada op. 8, *Rosza 1912, Zenemukiakó Vállalat, Budapest 1955*
Wildgans, F., 2 Konzert, *Doblinger*
Wissmer, 1960, *Ric*
Ziems, H., Kammerkonzert, 1962, für Klarinette und Streicher, *Br & H*

2 Concertos for several solo instruments including the clarinet

André, P., Concertino (2 Cl), *Deplaix*
Baur, J., Concertino, 1959 (Fl, Ob, Cl), *Br & H*
  Pentagramm, 1966 (Fl, Ob, Cl, Cor, Fag), *Br & H*
Beckerath, A. v., Doppelkonzert (Fl, Cl), *Sikorski*
Berger, A., Serenade concertante (Fl, Ob, Cl, Fag, V), *Peters*
Blacher, B., Konzertstück für Bläserquintett und Streichorchester, *B & B*
Bohne, R., Serenade op. 35 (Cl, Cor), *Benjamin*
Burghauser, J., Konzert (Fl, Ob, Cl, Fag, Cor), *Bä*
Buschmann, R., Concerto piccolo für Jazzquartett und Streicher (Cl,
  Guitar, Cb, Batt), *Bä*
Chevreuille, R., Concerto pour trio d'anches (Ob, Cl, Fag) et Orch.,
  Cebedem
Cikker, J., Erinnerungen (Fl, Ob, Cl, Fag, Cor), *Bä*
Dobiáš, V., Sonata (Fl, Ob, Cl, Fag, Cor, P, String Orchestra, Timp),
  Artia, Prague
Ferency, O., Serenade (Fl, Cl, Fag), *Bä*
Flothuis, M., Sonfonietta concertante (Cl, A-Sax), *Donemus*
Hindemith, P., Concerto (Fl, Ob, Cl, Fag, Harp), *Schott*
Holbrooke, J., Quadruple Concerto (Fl, Ob, Cl, Fag), *de Wolfe*
Kramář, F., Konzert für 2 Cl, *Bä*
Martelli, H., Concertino op. 85 (Ob, Cl, Cor, Fag, String Orch.), *Ric*
  Konzert für Cl und Fag, *Moeck*

Mozart, W. A., Sinfonia Concertante (version for Ob, Cl, Cor, Fag), *Br & H*
Quinet, M., Concertino, 1960 (Ob, Cl, Fag), *Cebedem*
   Concerto grosso (4 Cl), *Cebedem*
Ravel, M., Introduction et Allegro (Fl, Cl, Harp, Strings), *Durand*
Schäffer, B., Concerto per sei e tre (Cl, Sax, V, Vc, Continuo, P), *PMK*
Stamitz, K., Konzert B-Dur für Cl und Fag, *Sikorski, McGinnis & Marx*
Strauss, R., Concertino für Cl und Fag, *Hawkes 1944*
Tomasi, H., Divertimento corsica (Ob, Cl, Fag, Strings), *Leduc 1952*
Vivaldi, A., 2 Concerti in C-Dur (2 Ob, 2 Cl in C, Strings, Cembalo)
   Concerto in C 'per la Solennità di S. Lorenzo' (2 Fl, 2 Ob, 2 Cl in C,
     Fag, 2 V, Strings, Cembalo), *Ric*
Winter, P. v., Concertino (Cl, Vc), *Sikorski*

B   Clarinets only

1 *One clarinet*

Apostel, H. E., Sonatine op. 1912, *Universal 1951*
Baird, T., 2 Caprices, 1954, *PSPH*
Baur, J., 6 Bagatellen (Vogelrufe), *Br & H*
Bentzon, Tema med variationer op. 14 *Hansen 1929*
Blatt, 12 Capricen op. 17, *Ric*
Cavallini, E., Capricen, *Hofmeister, Ric*
Gambaro, J. B., 12 Capricen op. 18, *Schmidt, Ric*
Gambaro, V., 21 Capricci, *Ric*
   10 Caprices, *Doblinger*
Hartzell, E., Sonatine, *Doblinger*
Karg-Elert, S., Sonate op. 110, *Grahl & Nicklas*
Krenek, Monolog, *Bä*
Kunc, Pastoral Fantasy, *Peters*
Laderman, Serenade, *Peters*
Linke, N., Fantasia, *Gerig*
Lorenzo, L. de, Suite mythologique op. 38, *Grahl & Nicklas*
Lourié, The Mime, *Peters*
Magnani, A., 3 Sonates, *Evette*
Martino, D., A Set for Clarinet, *McGinnis & Marx 1957*
Osborne, Rhapsody, *Peters*
Pfeiffer, H., Musik für A-Cl, *Lienau 1937, McGinnis & Marx*
Pousseur, H., Madrigal I, *UE*
Rosza, Sonatine op. 27, *Peters*
Ruggiero, G., 20 Divertimenti, *Sikorski*
   6 Capricen, *Sikorski*

Rychlik, J., Burleske Suite, *Artia, Prague*
Smith, W. O., 5 Pieces, *UE*
   Variants, *UE*
Stravinsky, I., 3 Pieces, *Chester 1919*
Sutermeister, H., Capriccio, *Schott*
Tailleferre, Sonate, *Peters*
Wellesz, Suite op. 74, *Peters*

2 Duets for clarinets

Bach, C. P. E., Duett, *Nagel;* in Klar.-Duette aus der Frühzeit des
   Instrumentes, *Br & H*
Bacon, The Cockfight, *Peters*
Devienne, F., 6 Duos op. 76, *André*
   2 Duos concertants, *Doblinger*
Elton, A., Short Sonata, *Chester 1956*
Gebauer, F. R., 6 konzertante Duos op. 2 für 2 Cl, *Sikorski*
Hess, Duos, *Hinrichsen 1955*
Klug, E., Divertimento ticinese, *Heinrichshofen*
Lahusen, Pfeifermusik, *Br & H*
Maschayeki, A., 9 Expressionen (Cl, Bcl), *UE*
Mirandolle, L., 3 Duos, *Leduc*
Nocentini, D., 14 Duetti, *Carisch*
Poulenc, F., Sonata (A- and B-Cl), *Chester 1918*
Rousseau, J. J., Duette, in Klar.-Duette aus der Frühzeit des
   Instrumentes, *Br & H*
Schuller, G., Duo Sonata (Cl, Bcl), *Peters*
Wiedemann, L., 30 leichte Duette, *Benjamin*

3 Three clarinets

Blatt, *Ric*
Bove, J. H., Andante & Allegro (2 Cl, Bcl), *Leeds*
Carulli, *Ric*
Cooke, A., Suite, *OUP*
Donato, A., 3 Stücke, *UE*
   Pastorale and Dance, *Schirmer*
Mihalovici, M., Sonate op. 35 (Eb-Cl, A-Cl, Bcl), *Salabert 1933*
Müller, I., *Ric*
Pauer, J., Divertimento, 1948, *Bä*
Piket, F., Legend and Jollity, *Omega*
Stark, R., Sonate G-moll (2 Cl, Bh), *Schmidt 1897*
Townsend, Ballet Suite, *Peters*
Tuthill, B., Intermezzo op. 1/2, 1927 (2 Cl, Bh), *C. Fischer 1932*

4 *Four Clarinets*

Bozza, E., Andante und Scherzo, *Leduc*
Brown, T., Pieces, *Schirmer 1949*
Dillon, R., Marsch, *By & H*
   Allegro Festoso, *By & H*
   4 Quartette, *P. A. Schmidt*
Frangkiser, C., Star at Dawn, *By & H*
   Fugue à la valse, *By & H*
   Mélodie petite, *Pro Art*
Grundman, C., Bagatelle, *By & H*
   Caprice, *By & H*
Jelinek, H., Divertimento op. 15/8 (E♭-Cl, Cl, Bh, Bcl), *UE*
Keith, G. D., Interlude, *By & H*
Knighton, M., Kleines Menuett, *By & H*
   Quartet, *By & H*
   March Miniature, *By & H*
Kraehenbuehl, D., Variationen über eine Pavane für Krummhörner
   (Schein) (3 Cl, Bcl), *AMP*
Krenek, Tanz, *Belwin 1939*
McKay, G. F., On a Pastoral Theme, *Universal*
Piket, F., Reflection and Caprice, *Omega*
Quinet, Petite Suite, 1959, *Cebedem*
Rathaus, K., Country Serenade, *By & H*
Schoemaker, M., Volière, 1961, *Cebedem*
Stark, R., Serenade (2 Cl, Bh, Bcl), *Schmidt 1922*
Uhl, A., Divertimento (3 Cl, Bcl), *Schott 1957*
Waterson, J., Grand Quartet, *Mahillon, Andraud*
White, C. C., Suite Spirituale, *Elkan*
Wilson, K. A., Variations on a Theme of Paganini, *By & H*

5 *Five or more clarinets*

Meulemans, A., Rapsodie, 1961 (3 Cl, Bcl, A-Sax), *Cebedem*
Mozart, W. A., Adagio K. 411 (2 Cl, 3 Bh), *Br & H*
Schmitt, F., Sextett für 6 Cl (E♭-Cl, 2 B-Cl, Alt-Cl in E♭, Bcl, Cb Cl in E♭),
   Durand
Verrall, J., Serenade (3 Cl, Alt-Cl, Bcl), *UE*

C   Clarinet and Piano

Adaiewski, E., Sonate grecque, *Tischer & Jagenberg 1913*
d'Allessandro, R., Sonatina giocosa, *Gerig*

Alwyn, W., Sonata, *By & H*
Ameller, Cantilène, *Leduc*
Arnold, M., Sonatina op. 29, *Lengnick 1951*
Babin, V., Hillandale Waltzes, *By & H 1947*
Bacewicz, G., Leichte Stücke, *PMK*
Baermann, C., Zahlreiche Stücke für Cl und Klavier, *André, Schott*
Baird, T., 2 Capricen, *PMK*
Baklanowa, A., 8 leichte Stücke, *Hofmeister*
Barat, Chant slave, *Leduc*
   Fantaisie romantique, *Leduc*
   Pièce, *Leduc*
   Solo de Concours, *Leduc*
Bariller, Arlequinada, *Leduc*
Bárta, L., Sonate, *Artia, Prague*
Baur, J., Ballata Romana, *Br & H*
Bax, A., Sonata, *Murdoch 1935*
Beaucamp, Pièces romantiques, *Leduc*
Benjamin, A., Le Tombeau de Ravel, *By & H*
Berg, A., 4 Stücke op. 5, *UE 1920*
Bernaud, Concerto lyrique, *Leduc*
Bernstein, L., Sonate, *Witmark 1943*
Berr, A., Instruktive Variationen, *Hofmeister*
Bitsch, M., Pièces romantiques, *Leduc*
Bjelinski, B., Sonata, 1966, *Gerig*
Blémant, L., Bolero, *Leduc*
   Sous les sapins, *Leduc*
Bonneau, Suite, *Leduc*
Bozza, Fantaisie italienne, *Leduc*
   Bucolique, *Leduc*
   Aria, *Leduc*
   Claribel, *Leduc*
Brahms, J., Sonate F-moll op. 120, 1,
   Sonate E♭-Dur op. 120, 2, *By & H, Simrock*
Browne, P., A Trurd Maggot, *Hawkes 1944*
Burt, F., Duo, *UE*
Busoni, F., Elégie, *Br & H 1921*
Busser, Andante aus op. 22, *Leduc*
   Aragon op. 91, *Leduc*
   Cantegril op. 72, *Leduc*
   Pastorale op. 46, *Leduc*
Cahuzac, L., Fantasie variée, *Hansen 1947*
Cardew, P., Scherzo, 1954, *By & H*
Carter, E., Pastorale, *UE*

Castérède, J., Sonate, *Leduc 1957*
Cattolica, Duo, *Ric 1959*
Cavallini, E., Elégie, *Ric*
  Carnevale di Venezia (E♭-Cl), *Lienau*
  Adagio e Tarantella, *Ric*
Chevreuille, R., Récit. et air gai, 1950, *Cebedem*
Clérisse, Promenade, *Leduc*
  Vieille Chanson, *Leduc*
Clifton, Chalmers, Imtermezzo and Humoresque, *Le Roy 1926*
Coquard, Mélodie et Scherzetto op. 68, *Leduc*
Cundick, R., Turnabouts, *By & H*
Danzi, F., Sonate B-Dur, *Simrock*
Dautremer, M., Récit. et impromptu, *Leduc*
Debussy, C., Petite pièce, *Durand 1910*
Dervaux, P., Badinerie, *Leduc*
  Complainte, *Leduc*
Desenclos, A., D'un troubadour, *Leduc*
Dessau, Variationen über ein nordamerikanisches Volkslied, *Peters*
Dewanger, A., Ballade op. 88, *Leduc*
Dondeyn, Concertino, *Leduc*
Driessler, J., 5 Stücke op. 24/3a, *Bä*
Dubois, P. M., Romance, *Leduc 1957*
  Sonatina, *Leduc 1956*
Dunhill, T., Phantasy Suite op. 91, *Hawkes 1941*
Eder, H., Sonatine op. 34/5, *Doblinger*
Edmunds, C., Highland Croon, *Schott*
  Gay Hornpipe, *Schott*
  Lament, *Schott*
Ferguson, H., 4 Short Pieces, *Hawkes 1937*
Finke, F. F., Sonate, 1950, *Br & H*
Finzi, G., 5 Bagatelles, *Hawkes 1945*
Flosman, O., Sonatina, *McGinnis & Marx*
Gade, N. W., Fantasiestücke op. 43, *Br & H 1864, Augener*
Gagnebin, Andante und Allegro, *Leduc*
Gallois Montbrun, Concertstück, *Leduc*
  Humoresque, *Leduc*
  6 Pièces musicales d'études, *Leduc 1957*
Giampieri, Carnevale di Venezia, *Ric*
  Fantasie, *Ric*
Gibbs, A., *OUP*
Glière, R., 2 morceaux op. 35, Nr. 6 & 7, *Jurgenson*
Goedicke, A. F., 2 Stücke, *UE 1947*
Goepfart, O., Andante religioso op. 22, *Grahl & Nicklas*

Gordon, P., Sonatine, *UE*
Gouvy, T., Sonate op. 67, *Richault 1882, Costallat*
Gretchaninov, A. T., Suite miniature op. 145, *Leduc 1938*
Grovlez, Lamento et Tarantelle, *Leduc*
    Sarabande et Allegro, *Leduc*
Guillaume, M., Capriccietto, Canzona, Saltarello, op. 23, *Brogneaux*
Hamilton, I., 3 Nocturnes op. 6, 1951, *Schott*
    Sonata op. 22, *Schott 1957*
Hartig, H. F., Sonate op. 7, 1952, *B & B*
Heider, W., Dialog I, *Peters*
Herberigs, R., Sonatine, *Cebedem*
Hidas, F., Fantasie, *EMB*
Hill, E. B., Sonate op. 32, *Schirmer 1926/27*
Hindemith, P., Sonate, *Schott 1940*
Holbrooke, H., Andante and Presto op. 6/2, *Hawkes 1908*
    4 Mezzotints op. 55, *Cary*
    Nocturne, *Modern Music Library*
Honegger, A., Sonatine (A-Cl), *Rouart, Lerolle 1925*
Hopkins, A., Fantasy, *Chester 1951*
Howells, H., Sonata, *By & H 1954*
Hugon, G., Scherzo, *Costallat 1951*
Hunt, R., Meditation, *By & H*
Ibert, Aria (A-Cl), *Leduc*
Ireland, J., Fantasy Sonata, *By & H 1945*
Jacob, G., Sonatine, *Novello*
Jeanjean, P., Arabesques, *Andrieu 1926*
    Andantino, *Leduc*
    Prélude et Scherzo, *Leduc*
Jettel, R., Sonate, *Hofmeister*
Jongen, L., Pastorales et Gigue, *Brogneaux 1955*
Juchelka, M., Sonatine, *Artia, Prague*
Juon, P., Sonate op. 82 (A♭), *Schlesinger 1924*
Karg-Elert, S., Sonate op. 139b, *Zimmermann 1924*
Kaufmann, A., op. 48 Schipot, *Doblinger*
    op. 53 Sonatine, *Doblinger*
Kempter, L., Fantasie, *Schott*
Kennaway, L , Air, *Schott*
Klosé, Concertino, Airs variées, Soli, Pensées musicales, *Leduc*
Koechlin, C., 2 Sonaten, *Oiseau Lyre 1949*
Korda, V., Novelette, *Doblinger*
Kořinek, M., Sonatine, *Artia, Prague*
Kubizek, A., Sonatine op. 5a, *Doblinger*
Kummer, H., 7 Stücke op. 33, *Grahl & Nicklas*

Ladmirault, P., Sonate, *Leduc*
Laparra, R., Prélude, Valse et Irish Reel, *Leduc*
Laurischkus, M., Miniaturen op. 4 und op. 30, *Simrock*
Le Boucher, M., Fantaisie concertante, *Leduc*
   Ballade (D-minor), 1933, *Costallat*
Lecail, Fantaisie concertante (E♭-Cl), *Leduc*
Lefebvre, C., Fantaisie-Caprice op. 118, *Leduc*
Lefèvre, J. X., 5me Sonate, *Richli 1949*
   3me Sonate, *Richli 1949*
Legley, V., Sonate op. 40/3, 1952, *Cebedem*
Lethiere, C., Romance and Pollacca, *UE*
   Andante and Polonaise, *By & H*
Liadov, A., Prelude op. 46, 1899, *Moscow 1955*
Litaize, G., Récitatif et thème varié, *Leduc*
Lloyd, C. H., Suite in Olden Style, *Hawkes 1914*
Lothar, Sonate op. 74, *Bä*
Lovelock, W., *By & H*
Lutosławski, W., Prelude 1954, *PSPH*
Magnani, A., Mazurka-Caprice, *Leduc*
   2 Divertissements, *Leduc*
   Solo de Concert, *Leduc*
Martinu, B., Sonatina, *Leduc 1957*
Martelli, H., Preambule et Scherzo, 1945, *Costallat*
Marty, G., 1re Fantaisie, *Leduc*
Mason, D. G., Sonate op. 14, *Schirmer, Ditson 1920*
Mawet, L., Pièce lyrique, *Leduc*
Mendelssohn-Bartholdy, F., Sonate, *Sprague-Coleman, Leeds 1941*
Messager, Solo de Concours, *Leduc*
Meulemans, A., Sonata concertante 1948, *Cebedem*
   Rhapsodie, *Gervan*
Milford, R., Lyrical Movement, *OUP*
Milhaud, D., Sonatine, *Durand 1927*
Mirandole, L., Sonatine, *Leduc 1940*
   Sonate, *Leduc 1940*
Moeschinger, A., Sonatina op. 65, *By & H 1947*
Moritz, Edv., Pavane, *Grahl & Nicklas*
Moszkowski, Spanische Tänze, *Peters*
Moulaert, R., Rhapsodie écossaise, 1940, *Cebedem*
Mouquet, J., Solo de Concours, *Leduc*
Murrill, H., Prelude, Cadenza, Fugue, *OUP 1933*
Neubauer, F., Poetische Studien op. 10, *Hofmeister*
Osieck, H., Sonatine, *Donemus*
Oubadros, F., Cadence et divertissement, *Oiseau Lyre*

Pennequin, Cantilène et danse, *Leduc*
   Légende, *Leduc*
Perrier, Thème varié et presto, *Leduc*
Perry, H., Concertino, *By & H*
Phillips, G., Air, *Schott*
Pierné, G., Canzonetta op. 19, *Leduc*
   Serenade op. 7, *Leduc*
Piggott, Fantaisie in E♭, *Leduc 1954*
Pobjoy, V., 4 Stücke, *Schott 1957*
Poot, M., Arabesque, *Leduc*
   Ballade, *Vriamont*
Pratt, A., Idylle printanière, *Hawkes 1913*
   Souvenir d'Ispahan, *Hawkes 1913*
Quinet, M., Ballade, 1961, *Cebedem*
Rabaud, Solo de Concours op. 10, 1901, *Leduc*
Rainier, P., Suite (A-Cl), *Schott 1945*
Rakow, N., Sonate, *Sikorski*
Raphael, G., Enten-Sonatine op. 65, 1948, *Br & H*
Raybould, C., The Wistful Shepherd, *OUP 1939*
Reger, M., 2 Sonaten A♭-Dur und F♯-moll op. 49, 1 and 2, *UE 1903*
   Sonate B-Dur op. 107, *B & B 1909*
   Romanze in G, *Br & H*
Reiner, K., 4 Stücke, *Bä*
Revel, Fantaisie, *Leduc 1957*
Richardson, A., Roundelay, *OUP*
   3 Pieces, *Augener*
Riethmüller, H., Sonate op. 36, *Peters*
Risinger, K., Marionetten-Suite, *Bä*
Rochberg, G., Dialoge, *UE*
Rougnon, P., 1er Solo, *Leduc*
   Ballade, *Evette*
Rousseau, N., Sonatine op. 59, 1956, *Cebedem*
Rungis, R., 7 pièces, *Lemoine 1937*
Saint-Saëns, C., Sonate op. 167 in E♭, *Durand 1924*
Samuel, H., 3 Light Pieces (A-Cl), *Hawkes 1913*
Scharres, C., Cadence et Allegro apassionato, *Brogneaux 1956*
Schmid, H. K., Allegretto op. 34/2, *Schott*
Schmidek, K., Sonatine, *Doblinger*
Schmit, C., Prelude, *Leduc 1953*
Schmitt, F., Andantino op. 30, *Leduc*
Schollum, R., Sonatine op. 42/1, *Doblinger*
   Sonatine op. 55/4, *Doblinger*
Schumann, R., Phantasiestücke op. 37 (A-Cl), *Augener, Br & H, Peters*
Seiber, M., Andantino Pastorale, *Schott 1950*

Semler-Collery, J., Reverie et Scherzo, *Leduc 1955*
Serocki, K., Tanz, 1955, *PSPH*
Setacciolo, G., Sonate op. 31, *Ric 1921*
Shaw, C., Sonata, *Novello*
Sowerby, L , Sonata, *SPAM 1939*
Spinner, L., Suite op. 10, *By & H*
Stanford, C. V., Sonata op. 129, *Stainer & Bell 1918*
  3 Intermezzi op. 13, *Novello 1880*
Stark, R., Romanze op. 1, *Schmidt*
  4 Stücke op. 19, *Schmidt*
Štastný, V., Concertino, *Artia, Prague*
Steffens, W., Hommage à Bartók, *Br & H*
Stevens, H., Suite, *Peters*
Stouffer, P. M., Recitation, *Benjamin*
Stürmer, B., Sonate op. 73, *Süddeutscher Musikverlag*
Szabó, F., Sonata alla Rapsodia, *EMB*
Szalowski, A., Sonatina, *Omega 1948*
Taneiev, S., Arabesque, *Andrieu*
  Sonate, *Benjamin*
Taubert, K. H., Französische Skizzen, *Benjamin*
Templeton, A., 1. Pocket-Size-Sonata, *Leeds*
  2. Pocket-Size-Sonata, *Templeton 1956*
Tomasi, H., Introduction et danse, *Leduc*
  Complainte du jeune Indien, *Leduc*
  Chant corse, *Leduc 1949*
Tovey, D., Sonate op. 16, *Schott 1912*
Tuthill, B. C., Fantasy Sonata op. 3, *Fischer 1936*
Vassilenko, S., Rhapsodie Orientale, *Benjamin*
Vinter, G., Concertino, *By & H*
Vlag, H., Ballade, *Heuwekemeijer*
Vostřak, Z., Burleske, *Artia, Prague*
Wagner, J., Konzertstück, *By & H*
Walker, R., Moment Musical, *UE*
Walter, F., 2 Fantasiestücke, *Grahl & Nicklas*
Walthew, R., Suite in F, *Boosey 1899*
  Mosaic in 10 pieces, *Boosey 1900*
  4 Meditations, *Boosey 1897/1903*
Wanhal, J., *McGinnis & Marx 1948*
Webber, L., Air and Variations, 1952, *Francis*
  Theme and Variations, 1952, *Francis*
Webber, R., Romany Caprice, *UE*
Weber, C. M. v., Grand Duo concertant op. 47, *Lemoine, By & H, Lienau*, etc.
  Variationen op. 33, *Lienau, Peters*

Weinberger, J., Sonatine, *Fischer 1940*
Weiner, L., Ballade op. 8, *Rózsavölgyi 1912*
  Peregi Verbunk, *Zenemukiakó Vállalat*
Weis, F., Sonate (A-Cl), 1935, *Kistner, DFM*
Wellesz, E., 2 Stücke op. 34 (A-Cl), 1922, *UE*
Wildgans, F., Vortragsstücke op. 14/3, *UE*
  Sonatine, *Doblinger*
Wirth, H., Sonate (A-Cl), *Sikorski*
Wordsworth, W., Prelude & Scherzo op. 52, *Benjamin*
Wuille, Fantasie, *Ric 1951*
Zieritz, G. v., Musik, *Grahl & Nicklas*
Zilcher, H., Schmerzliches Adagio op. 49, *Br & H*

D Duets for Clarinet and String Instrument

1 Duets for clarinet and violin

Bentzon, J., Intermezzo op. 24, *Hansen*
Berg, G., 1947, *DFM*
Busch, A., Hausmusik, op. 26/1 & 2, *Br & H 1926*
Hindemith, P., 2 Stücke, *Schott 1932*
Raphael, G., Duo op. 47/6, *Süddeutscher Musikverlag*

2 Duets for clarinet and other string instrument or harp

Berezowsky, N., Duo op. 15 (Cl, Va), *Leeds*
David, J. N., Sonate op. 32/4 (Cl, Va), *Br & H*
Leerink, H., Sonata op. 19 (Cl, Vc), *Donemus*
Poenitz, F., Capriccio op. 73 (Cl, Harp), *Br & H 1905*
Tate, P., Sonata (Cl, Vc), *OUP 1949*

E Duets for Clarinet and Another Wind Instrument

1 Duets for clarinet and flute

Burkhard, W., Serenade, *Bä*
Kisiliewski, S., Suite, *PMK*
Krenek, Sonatina, *Bä*
Michael, Sonatine, *Ric*
Moszumanska-Nazar, K., 5 Duette, *PMK*
Riegger, W., Duo op. 35/2, *UE*
Szalowski, A., Duo, *Omega 1948*
Villa-Lobos, H., Chôros, No. 2, *Eschig 1927*

2 *Duets for clarinet and oboe*

Bauer, M., op. 25, *Peters*
Berger, A., *Peters*
Høffding, F., Dialoger, *SM 1944*
Phillips, G., Suite, *Schott 1950*
Riegger, W., Duo op. 35/3, *UE*
Wigglesworth, F., Duo, *UE*

3 *Duets for clarinet and bassoon*

Beethoven, L. van, 3 Duos op. 147, *Br & H, Schmidt, André, Hofmeister*
Defossez, R., Duo, *Brogneaux*
Fernandez, O. L., 3 Invencos, *Southern Music Co.*
Gebauer, F. R., 6 Konzertante Duos op. 8, *Sikorski*
Gramatges, H., Prelude and Invention, 1941, *Southern Music Co.*
Haan, H. de, Divertimento, *Hinrichsen*
Kunert, K., Sonate op. 15, *Hofmeister 1954*
Poulenc, F., Sonate, *Chester 1922*

4 *Duets for clarinet and horn*

Dobrzynski, I. F., Duo, *PMK*
Wildgans, F., 3 Inventionen, *Doblinger*

F Trios for Clarinet, Piano and String Instrument

1 *Trios for piano, clarinet and violin*

Bartók, B., Contrasts, *By & H 1942*
Baussnern, W. v., Serenade in E♭, *Simrock 1905*
Berg, A., Adagio, *UE*
Ives, C., Largo, *Southern Music Co.*
Khachaturian, A., Trio, *Anglo-Soviet 1932*
Krenek, E., Trio, 1946, *AMP*
Mason, D. G., Pastorale op. 8, *Mathot 1913*
Milhaud, D., Suite, *Senart 1937*
Riethmüller, H., op. 46, *Sikorski*
Stravinsky, I., Suite de l'Histoire du Soldat, *Chester 1920*
Tate, P., Air and Variations, *OUP*
Walthew, R., Trio, *Boosey 1897*

2 *Trios for piano, clarinet and viola*

Amberg, J., Fantasiestücke op. 12, *Hansen 1910*
Bruch, M., 8 Stücke, op. 83, *Simrock 1910*
Holbrooke, J., Nocturne op. 51/1, *Chester*
Juon, P., Trio-Miniaturen, *Lienau*
Mozart, W. A., Kegelstatt-Trio K. 498, *Br & H*
Reinecke, C., Trio op. 264, *Simrock*
Schumann, R., Märchenerzählungen op. 132, *Br & H*
Uhl, A., Kleines Konzert, *Doblinger*

3 *Trios for piano, clarinet and cello (or double bass)*

Amberg, J., Trio op. 11, *Hansen 1912*
   Fantasiestücke op. 12, *Hansen 1910*
Beethoven, L. van, Gassenhauer-Trio op. 11, *Br & H*
   Trio op. 38, *Br & H* (arranged by Beethoven himself)
Blomdahl, K. B., *Schott*
Brahms, J., Trio op. 114, *Simrock 1892, Peters*
Busch, A., Deutsche Tänze, *Br & H*
Frühling, C., op. 40, *Leuckart*
Gramatges, H., Trio, 1944, *Southern Music Co.*
Grovermann, C. H., Trio in B, *Sander 1940*
d'Indy, V., Trio op. 29, *Hamelle 1887*
Juon, P., Trio-Miniaturen, *Lienau 1941*
Kahn, R., Trio op. 45, *Schlesinger*
Koetsier, J., Trio op. 13/2, *Donemus*
Krejci, I., Trio (Cl, Cb, P), *Artia, Prague 1937*
Kubizek, A., op. 26a, *Doblinger*
Lefèvre, J. X., Sonates 2 & 3, *Richli*
Raphael, G., Trio op. 70, *Br & H*
Zemlinsky, A., Trio op. 3, *Simrock 1897*
Zilcher, H., Trio op. 90, *Süddeutscher Musikverlag*

G Trios for Piano, Clarinet and Another Wind Instrument

1 *Trios for piano, clarinet and flute*

Cole, H., Trio, *Novello 1955*
Emmanuel, M., Trio-Sonate, *Durand*
Grundman, C., Waltz and Interlude, *By & H*
Saint-Saëns, C., Serenade
   Tarantelle op. 6, *Durand*
Schmitt, F., Sonatine en trio, *Durand 1935*
Tscherepnin, I., Cadenzas, *Belaieff*

2 *Trios for piano, clarinet and bassoon*

Bach, C. P. E., 6 Sonaten (Cl, Fag, Cembalo), *EMB*
Dessau, Variationen über 'Hab mein Wagen vollgeladen', *Peters*
Glinka, M., Trio pathétique, *Jurgenson 1827, Musica Rara*
Kreutzer, C., Trio op. 43, *Hofmeister*
Roetscher, K., Risser-Trio op. 29, *B & B*

3 *Trios for piano, clarinet and another wind instrument*

Kopsch, J., Trio (Ob, Cl, P), *UE*
Mendelssohn-Bartholdy, F., 2 Konzertstücke op. 113, 114 (Cl, Bh, P),
    Br & H, Internat. Music Co. 1957
Reinecke, C., Trio op. 247 (Cl, Cor, P), *Senff*
Tovey, D., Trio op. 8 (Cl, Cor, P), *Schott 1906*

H   Wind Trios

1 *Trios for flute, clarinet and bassoon*

Apostel, H. E., 5 Bagatellen op. 20, *UE*
Bentzon, J., Sonatine op. 7, *SM*
Biersack, A., Divertimento, 1908, *Schott*
Borris, S., Terzettino, *Sirius*
Brero, Trio-Divertimento, *Ric*
Eder, H., Wächter-Divertimento, *Heinrichshofen*
Fritter, J., 8 Rondels, *UE*
de Haan, S., Trio, *Schott 1951*
Keldorfer, R., Trio, *Doblinger*
Ketting, P., *Donemus*
Kochan, Divertimento op. 12, *Peters*
Koechlin, C., Trio op. 92 in G, *Senart, Salabert 1928, Ric*
Kötschau, Divertimento op. 12a, *Peters*
Lorenzo, L. de, op. 76 Trio Eccentrico, *Peters*
    2 Divertimenti op. 24, 29, *Zimmermann 1931*
Moeschinger, A., 5 Capricci, *Heinrichshofen*
Moritz, E., Divertimento op. 150, *Grahl & Nicklas*
Peeters, op. 80, *Peters*
Pijper, W., *Donemus, Peters*
Poot, M., Divertimento, *Eschig 1958*
Urbanner, E., 8 Aphorismen, *Doblinger*
Vogler, E., Die kleine Stadt, *Br & H*
Walckiers, E., 3 Trios, *Richault*
Weis, F., Musik, *Kistner 1930, DFM*

Wildgans, F., Kleines Trio, *Doblinger*
Willbrandt, Osteuropäische Lieder und Tänze, *Peters*

2 Trios for flute, oboe and clarinet

Arnold, M., Divertimento op. 37, *Paterson* 1952
Bennett, R. R., Trio, *UE*
Carion, F., Bagatelles op. 19, *Brogneaux 1948*
Doppelbauer, J. F., Trio I, *Doblinger*
Flothuis, M., Nocturne op. 11 (A-Cl), *Chester 1952*
Goeb, R., Suite, *Peer 1952*
Görner, H. G., Trio op. 24, *Simrock*
Nilsson, B., 20 Gruppen (Piccolo, Ob, Cl), *UE*
Shostakovich, D., Preludes, *Edition Musicus, New York*

3 Trios for oboe, clarinet and bassoon (Trio d'anches)

Arrieu, C., *Amphion 1948*
Auric, G., *Oiseau Lyre 1948*
Badings, H., *Donemus*
Baeyens, A., Concertino, 1951, *Metropolis*
Barraud, H., *Oiseau Lyre 1938*
Bartoš, F., *Artia, Prague*
Bauernfeind, H., Heitere Musik, *Doblinger*
Baumann, H., Divertimento, *Sikorski*
Bentzon, J., Racconto nr. 3, op. 31, *SM*
Bertouille, G., Prélude et fugue, 1957, *Cebedem*
Bonneau, P., 3 Noëls anciens, *Leduc 1949*
Bourguignon, F. de, Suite en trio op. 80, 1944, *Cebedem*
Boutry, Divertimento, *Leduc*
Bozza, E., Suite brève, op. 67, *Leduc 1947*
    Fughette, Sicilienne & Rigaudon, *Leduc*
Chemin-Petit, H., Trio im alten Stil, *Lienau*
Constant, M., *Chester 1949*
Defossez, R., 1946, *Cebedem*
Delvaux, A., 1948, *Cebedem*
Desprez, F., Prélude & Danse, *Brogneaux 1950*
Escher, R., op. 4, *Donemus 1948*
Favre, G., Gouaches, *Durand 1957*
Ferroud, P. O., (A-Cl), *Durand 1934*
Flegier, Concert Suite, *Gallet 1897, Rubank*
Fontyn, J., 7 petites pièces, 1956, *Cebedem*
Foret, F., Suite en trio, *Costallat 1953*
Françaix, J., Divertissement, *Schott*

Höffer, P., Kleine Suite, *Sikorski*
   Thema mit Variationen, *Sikorski 1944*
Ibert, J., 5 pièces, *Oiseau Lyre*
   Andantino et Allegro marziale, *Leduc*
Ikonomov, B., op. 14, in E, *Oiseau Lyre 1937*
Jong, M. de, op. 126, 1961, *Cebedem*
Jongen, L., *Brogneaux*
Juon, P., Arabesques op. 73, *Lienau 1940*
Kelkel, Divertimento, *Ric*
Klein, R. R., Serenade, *Heinrichshofen*
Kurzbach, *Peters*
Legley, V., op. 11, 1942, *Brogneaux*
Lutosławski, W., *PSPH*
Maegaard, J., 1950, (A-Cl), *DFM*
Maintenon, J., Sonatine, *Costallat*
Maros, R., Serenade, *Zememukiakó Vallalat, Budapest*
Martelli, H., op. 45, *Costallat 1947*
Martinon, J., Sonatine nr. 4, *Costallat*
Martinu, B., 4 Madrigale, *Schott*
Meulemans, A., Trio, 1933, *Brogneaux 1950*
   2ᵉ Trio, 1960, *Cebedem*
Migot, G., (A-Cl), *Leduc 1946*
Milhaud, D., Suite d'après Corrette, *Oiseau Lyre 1938*
   Suite pastorale, *Senart 1937*
Pierné, P., Bucolique variée, *Costallat 1947*
Poulenc, F., *Hansen*
Rivier, J., Petite Suite, *Fougères*
Ropartz, G., Entrata e Scherzetto, *Salabert 1947*
Rousseau, N., Trios jouets op. 53, 1955, *Cebedem*
Roussel, A., Andante, *Leduc*
Sauguet, H., *Oiseau Lyre 1948*
Schiff, H., Divertimento, *Doblinger*
Schiske, K., op. 41, Triosante, *Doblinger*
Schmit, C., Trio, 1945, *Cebedem*
Schoemaker, M., Suite champêtre, 1940, *Cebedem*
Schulhoff, E., Divertissement, *Schott 1928*
Szalowski, A., *Chester 1948, Omega*
Székely, E., Divertimento, *EMB*
Tansman, A., Suite, *Eschig*
Tomasi, G., Concert champêtre, *Lemoine 1938*
Velden, R. van der, Divertimento, 1957, *Cebedem*
Villa-Lobos, H., Trio, 1921, *Eschig, Schott*
Walthew, R. H., Triolet, *By & H 1934*

Weber, A., Trio d'anches, *Leduc 1957*
Woestijne, D. van de, Divertimento, 1941, *Cebedem*

4 *Trios for two clarinets and bassoon*

Eisenmann, W., Divertimento, *Sikorski*
Jelinek, H., 6 Aphorismen op. 9/3, *UE*
Mason, J., Canonic Device, *Benjamin*
Mozart, W. A., 5 Divertimenti, edition for 3 Cl and Fag, *Br & H*

5 *Other wind trios*

Dressel, E., Trio miniature (Cl, Cor, Fag), *Ries & Erler*
Händel, G. F., Ouverture (2 Cl, Cor), *Schott 1952*
Karg-Elert, S., Trio op. 49 (Ob, Cl, CIngl), *Merseburger 1905*
Mozart, W. A., Kanonisches Adagio (2 Bh, Fag), *Br & H*
Regner, H., Divertimento (Fl, 2 Cl), *Heinrichshofen*
Stark, R., Sonate op. 55 (2 Cl, Bh), *Schmidt 1897*

J Trios for Wind, String and Other Instruments

Bentzon, J., Intermezzo (Fl, Cl, V), *Hansen*
Blumer, T., Trio op. 55 (Cl, V, Vc), *Simrock*
Busch, A., Deutsche Tänze op. 26/3 (Cl, V, Vc), *Br & H 1926*
Eklund, H., Liten Serenad (Cl, V, Cb), *Nordiska 1955*
Heidrich, M., Trio op. 33 (Cl, V, Va), *Schmidt*
Herold, E., Serenade (Cl, V, Va), *Schmidt*
Ingenhoven, J., Trio (Fl, Cl, Harp), *Senart 1920*
Jettel, R., Trio (Cl, V, Va), *Doblinger*
Juon, P., Divertimento op. 34 in D (Cl, 2 Va), *Schlesinger, Lienau*
Kelterborn, Lyrische Kammermusik (Cl, V, Va), *Bä*
Kramar, F., 13 pièces (2 Cl, Va) op. 47, *Ric*
Lampersberg, G., Trio (Cl, V, Tamb. picc.), *UE*
Markevitch, I., Serenade (Cl, V, Fag), *Schott 1931*
Nedbal, M. J. M., Kleines Trio (Cl, Fag, Vc), *Doblinger*
Pfister, H., Preambolo, Aria e Ballo (Cl, Guitar, Cb), *Heinrichshofen*
Schiske, K., Musik op. 27 (Cl, Tr, Va), *UE*
Stravinsky, I., Epitaph (Fl, Cl, Harp), *By & H*

K Quartets with Piano

Amberg, J., Suite (Fl, Ob, Cl, P), *Hansen 1905, Andraud*
Cailliet, L., Divertissement (3 Cl, P), *Elkan*
Casella, A., Sinfonia (Cl, Tr, Vc, P), *Carisch 1939*
Castéra, R. de, Concerto (Fl, Cl, Vc, P), *Rouart, Salabert*

Delvaux, A., Cinq impromptus (Ob, Cl, Fag P), 1949, *Cebedem*
Françaix, J., Quartet (Fl, Ob, Cl, P), *Andraud*
Hindemith, P., Quartet (Cl, V, Vc, P), *Schott 1938*
Honegger, A., Rhapsodie (2 Fl, Cl, P), 1917, *Senart 1923, Salabert*
Manicke, D., Quartett in D (Cl, Cor, Fag, P), *Simrock*
Messiaen, O., Quatuor pour la Fin du Temps (Cl, V, Vc, P), *Durand 1942*
Milhaud, D., Sonate (Fl, Ob, Cl, P), *Durand 1923*
Quinet, M., Concertino (Ob, Cl, Fag, P), 1960, *Cebedem*
Saint-Saëns, C., Caprice op. 79 (Fl, Ob, Cl, P), *Durand 1887*
Scherber, F., Quartett (Ob, Cl, Bcl, P), *Schmidt 1914*
Schmitt, F., À tour d'anches, op. 97 (Ob, Cl, Fag, P), *Durand 1943*
Webern, A., Quartett op. 22 (V, Cl in C, Ten-Sax, P), *UE 1932*

L Quartets for Clarinet and Strings
(violin, viola and cello)

Crusell, B., Quatuors, op. 2, 4, 7, *Peters c. 1820*
    Quatuor op. 2/1, *Ric*
David, T. C., Quartett, 1955, *Br & H*
Eder, H., Quartett, 1955, *Br & H*
Hindemith, P., Aus 'Plöner Musiktag', *Schott*
Hoffmeister, F. A., *Doblinger*
Hummel, J. H., *Musica Rara 1958*
Rawsthorne, A., *OUP 1950*
Stamitz, C., 6 Quatuors op. 8, *Sieber*
    Quatuor op. 8/4, *Raabe 1919, Afas*
    2 Quartette op. 14, *McGinnis & Marx*

M Wind Quartets

1 *Woodwind quartets (flute, oboe, clarinet, bassoon)*

Badings, H., 3 Niederländische Tänze, *Donemus*
Barbier, R., Petite suite op. 108, 1964, *Cebedem*
Berger, A., 1941, *Peters*
Bertouille, G., Prélude et fugue, 1959, *Cebedem*
Bitsch, M., Divertissement, *Leduc*
Blacher, B., Divertimento op. 38, *B & B 1951*
Bozza, 3 Stücke für eine Nachtmusik, *Leduc*
Bridge, F., Divertimenti, *By & H 1940*
Doppelbauer, J. F., *Doblinger*
Fernandez, O. L., Suite in F op. 37, *AMP*
Françaix, J., *Schott*
Grünauer, I., *Doblinger*

Helm, E., *Benjamin*
Jones, C., Lyric Waltz Suite, *Peters 1955*
Kabalevski, D., Kindersuite, op. 27, *Spratt*
Kay, N. F., Miniature Quartet, *OUP*
Lajtha, 4 Huldigungen, *Leduc*
Limmert, E., Griechische Essays, 1965, *Br & H*
Lorenzo, L. de, op. 80
    I Quattro Virtuosi, *Peters*
Malipiero, G. F., Sonata a quattro, *UE*
Meulemans, A., Quatuor, 1962, *Cebedem*
Mirandolle, L., Quartett, *Schott 1935*
Poot, M., Petite marche de fête, 1938, *Cebedem*
Quinet, M., 1964, *Cebedem*
Raphael, G., op. 61, *Süddeutscher Musikverlag*
Riisager, K., op. 40a, *DFM*
Schmit, C., Burlesques, *Cebedem*
Sontag, H. O., Quartet on Old Tunes, *UE*
Walentynowicz, W., Kleines Quartett im klassischen Stil, *PMK*
Wilkinson, P. G., Suite, *Novello*

2 *Quartets for other wind instruments*

Apostel, H. E., Quartett op. 14 (Fl, Cl, Cor, Fag), *UE*
Butt, J., Winsome's Folly (Ob, Cl, Cor, Fag), *By & H*
Chávez, C., Soli (Ob, Cl, Tr, Fag), *By & H*
Chwartz, L., Evening in the Turkestan Steppe (Fl, CIngl, Cl, Fag),
    Hawkes 1937
Cruft, A., Dance Movement (Fl, Ob, Cl, Cor), *Elkin*
Domansky, A., Divertimento (2 Cl, Cor, Fag), *Schmidt*
Ehrenberg, C., Quartet op. 40 (Ob, Cl, Cor, Fag), *Benjamin*
Haydn, J., Divertimento (2 Cl, 2 Cor), *Hansen 1932*, *Doblinger*
Ibert, J., 2 Mouvements (2 Fl, Cl, Fag), *Leduc 1923*
Korda, V., Etüde (Fl, Cl, Cor, Tr), *Doblinger*
Krejčí, I., Divertimento (Fl, Cl, Fag, Trbne), *Bä*
Mozart, Cassation (Ob, Cl, Cor, Fag), *Andraud*
Padovano, A., Rondo (Ob, Cl, Cor, Fag), *Sikorski*
Petyrek, F., Spielmusik über sudetendeutsche Volkslieder (Ob, Cl, Cor,
    Fag), *Doblinger*
Regner, Serenade (Ob, Cl, Cor, Fag), *Heinrichshofen*
Rossini, G., 6 Quartette (version for Fl, Cl, Cor, Fag), *Schott 1935*
Stamitz, K., Quartett op. 8/2 Eb-Dur (version for Ob, Cl, Cor, Fag;
    original Ob, Cor, Va, Fag) *Denkmäler der Tonkunst in Bayern XV*
Stark, R., Serenade op. 55 (2 Cl, Bh, Bcl), *Schmidt*
Sutermeister, H., Serenade (2 Cl in C, Tr, Fag), *Schott*

N Quartets for Wind Instruments with Strings or Harp, Guitar, Percussion

Dessau, P., Concertino (V, Va, Cl, Cor), *Schott*
Fritter, J., 8 Rondels (Fl, Cl, Fag, Va), *UE*
Lampersberg, G., Quartett (Fl, Bcl, Va, Guitar),
Maconchy, E., Reflections (Ob, Cl, Va, Harp), *OUP*
Migot, G., Quartett (Fl, Cl, V, Harp), *Sirène 1927, Leduc*
Moniuszko, S., Wilde Rose (Fl, 2 Cl, Cb), *PSPH 1955*
Pier, G., 3 Etüden (Cl, Tr, P, Tamb. picc.), *Doblinger*
Roetscher, K., Divertimento op. 22 (Fl, A-Cl, V, Vc), *B & B*
Sheinkman, Divertimento (Cl, Tr, Harp, Trbne), *Peters*
Vogel, W., 'Inspiré par Jean Arp' (Fl, Cl, V, Vc), *Heinrichshofen*
Wagner-Régeny, Divertimento (Fl, Cl, Fag, Batt), *Br & H*
Westergaard, P., Quartett (V, Vibr., Cl in A, Vc), *Ars Viva*

O Quintets with Piano

1 *Quintets for piano and wind instruments*

Abramsky, A., Concertino (Fl, Cl, Cor, Fag, P), *UE 1929*
Beethoven, L. van, op. 16 (Ob, Cl, Cor, Fag, P), *Br & H, André*
Danzi, F., Quintett op. 41 D-moll (Ob, Cl, Cor, Fag, P), *Benjamin*
Duncan, E., (Fl, Cl, Cor, Fag, P), *Rudall*
Gieseking, W., (Ob, Cl, Cor, Fag, P), *By & H*
Huybrechts, A., Suite (Fl, Ob, Cl, Fag, P), *1929, Cebedem*
Jongen, L., Quintuor (Fl, Cl, Cor, Fag, P), *1958, Cebedem*
Lees, B., 3 Variables (Ob, Cl, Cor, Fag, P), *By & H*
Mozart, W. A., K. 452 (Ob, Cl, Cor, Fag, P), *Br & H*
Rawsthorne, A., Quintet (Ob, Cl, Cor, Fag, P), *OUP*
Regamey, K., Quintett (Cl, Fag, V, Vc, P), *PMK*
Rimsky-Korsakov, N., (Fl, Cl, Cor, Fag, P), *Belaieff 1911*
Spohr, L., op. 52 (Fl, Cl, Cor, Fag, P), *Peters, Br & H*
Verhey, T., Quintett op. 20 (Ob, Cl, Fag, Cor, P), *Br & H*
Volbach, F., Quintett op. 24 (Ob, Cl, Fag, Cor, P), *Br & H*

2 *Quintets for piano, wind instruments and strings*

Dunhill, T. F., op. 3 (Cl, Cor, V, Vc, P), *Rudall 1913*
Fibich, Z., op. 42 (Cl, Cor, V, Vc, P), *Urbánek 1894*
Hauer, J. M., op. 26 (Cl, V, Va, Vc, P), *Lienau, Schlesinger 1924*
Hindemith, P., 3 Stücke op. 35 (Cl, Tr, V, Cb, P), *Schott 1925*
Huber, H., op. 136 (Fl, Cl, Cor, Fag, P), *Hug 1920*
Kahn, R., op. 54 (Cl, V, Cor, Vc, P), *B & B 1910*

Kopelent, M., Musik für Fünf (Ob, Cl, Fag, Va, P), *Gerig*
Magnard, A., op. 8 (Fl, Ob, Cl, Fag, P), *Rouart 1918, Salabert*
Shifrin, Serenade (Ob, Cl, Cor, Va, P), 1954, *Peters*
Weingartner, F., op. 50 (Cl, V, Va, Vc, P), *Br & H 1911*

P   Quintets for Clarinet and Strings
(two violins, viola and cello, unless otherwise stated)

Bliss, A., (A-Cl), *Novello 1933*
Brahms, J., (A-Cl), op. 115, *Simrock 1892, By & H*
Cooke, A., *By & H*
David, T. C., Quintett (Cl, V, Va, Vc, Cb), *Doblinger*
Fromm-Michaels, I., Musica larga, *Sikorski*
Fuchs, R., op. 102, *Robitschek 1919*
Goldberg, Th., op. 7, *B & B*
Hindemith, P., (B- and E♭-Cl), op. 30, *Schott 1922*
Hoesslin, F. v., (A-Cl), *Simrock 1924*
Holbrooke, J., op. 27/1, *Novello 1914*
    op. 27/2, *Chester 1914*
Höller, K., op. 46, *Süddeutscher Musikverlag*
Höller, K., op. 46, *Müller*
Horvitz, J., Concertante, *Chester 1953*
Howells, H., Rhapsodic Quintet op. 31, *Stainer & Bell 1921, Galaxy*
Jacob, G., *Novello 1946*
Kornauth, E., op. 33, *Doblinger*
Krehl, S., (A-Cl) op. 19, *Simrock 1902*
Landré, G., 4 Miniaturen, *Donemus*
Maconchy, E., *By & H*
Mozart, W. A., K. 581, *Br & H, By & H*
Müller, S. W., Divertimento op. 13, *Br & H 1927*
Raphael, G., Serenade op. 4, *Simrock 1925*
Reger, M., (A-Cl) op. 146, *Peters 1916, Simrock*
Reicha, A., Quintett B-Dur, *Benjamin*
Reizenstein, F., Thema, Variationen und Fuge op. 2, *Benjamin*
Spohr, L., Andante mit Variationen op. 34, *Schmidt*
Thilman, op. 73, *Peters*
Weber, C. M., Quintett op. 34, *Lienau, Costallat*
    Introduktion, Thema und Variationen, *Lienau*
Wellesz, E., op. 81, *Heinrichshofen*
Wordsworth, W., *Lengnick*

Q   Quintets for Flute, Oboe, Clarinet, Horn and Bassoon

Absil, J., op. 16, 1934, *Cebedem*

Angerer, P., *Doblinger*
Arnell, Cassation op. 45, *Peters*
Badings, H., Quintett Nr. 1, *Donemus 1929*
    Quintett Nr. 4, *Donemus 1949*
Baeyens, A., 1950, *Cebedem*
Bakaleinikov, V., Introduction and Scherzo, *Belwin*
Ballay, G., L'Aurore sur la Forêt (Cor solo), *Evette, Leduc*
    La Vallée silencieuse (Fl solo), *Evette, Leduc*
    Petite Suite Miniature, *Leduc 1948*
Ballif, C., op. 10, *B & B*
Barber, S., Summer Music op. 31, *G. Schirmer 1957*
Bartoš, F., Bürger als Edelmann, Suite, *Bä*
Baur, J., Quintetto sereno, *Br & H*
Bentzon, J., Racconto Nr. 5, *SM*
Berger, J., 6 kleine Stücke, *Grahl & Nicklas*
Bergmann, W., Musik, *Doblinger*
Birtwistle, H., Refrains and Choruses, *UE*
Bitsch, M., Sonatine, *Leduc*
Blumer, T., Suite, Serenade & Thema mit Var. op. 34, *Simrock 1919*
    Schweizer Quintett op. 52, 1924, *Sikorski*
    Tanzsuite op. 53, *Simrock 1925*
Borris, S., op. 25/2, *Sirius*
Bosmans, A., Diabelliana, Suite nach Diabelli, *Elkan*
Bourguignon, F. de, 2 pièces op. 71, 1941, *Cebedem*
Bozay, A., *EMB*
Bozza, E., Variations sur un thème libre, *Leduc 1943*
    Scherzo op. 48, *Leduc*
Brenta, G., Le Soldat Fanfaron, 1952, *Cebedem*
Brod, H., op. 2/1, *Hofmeister*
Brugk, H. M., Serenade op. 22, *Sikorski*
Bruns, V., op. 16, *Hofmeister 1954*
Burian, E. F., *Bä*
Cailliet, L., Concertino, *Elkan*
    Ouverture, *Elkan*

Carion, F., Fantaisie concertante, *Brogneaux 1951*
Carter, E., 1948, *AMP 1955*
Castérède, *Leduc 1955*
Chailley, Barcarole, *Leduc 1948*
Chemin-Petit, H., *Lienau*
Chevreuille, R., Divertissement, 1942, *Cebedem*
    Sérénade op. 65, 1956, *Cebedem*
Clapp, P. G., Prélude et Finale, *By & H*
Coker, W., *UE*

Dahl, I., Allegro Arioso, *Hofmeister*
Damase, J. M., 17 Variations op. 22, *Leduc 1952*
Danzi, F., op. 56/1 B-Dur, *Leuckart*
 op. 56/2 G-moll, *Br & H, Leuckart*
 op. 67/2 C-moll, *Ric*
 op. 68/1 A-Dur, *Ric*
 op. 68/2 F-Dur, *Ric*
Dávid, G., 2 Quintette, *EMB*
Dehnert, Festliche Musik, *Peters*
Dobiáš, V., Pastoral Quintett, *Artia, Prague*
Domansky, A., *Schmidt 1927*
Domenico, O., *Leduc 1955*
Douglas, R., 6 Dance Caricatures, *Hinrichsen 1950*
Dubois, P. M., Fantasia, *Leduc*
Eder, H., op. 25, *Doblinger*
Erdlen, H., Kleine Variationen op. 27/1, *Grahl & Nicklas*
Essex, K., *Hinrichsen*
Farkas, F., Serenade, *EMB*
Fine, I., Partita, 1948, *By & H*
Foerster, J. B., op. 95, *Hudebni Matice 1927*
Françaix, J., *Schott 1951*
Fricker, P. R., op. 5, *Schott 1951*
Fürst, P. W., Konzertante Musik op. 25, *Doblinger*
 op. 29, 3, *Doblinger*
Gayfer, J. M., Suite, *By & H*
Genzmer, 1956, *Peters*
Goeb, R., Prairie Songs, *Peer 1952*
 2 Quintette, *McGinnis & Marx*
Hamerik, E., *DFM*
Haufrecht, A Woodland Serenade, *Peters*
Heiden, B., Sinfonia, 1949, *AMP 1957*
Henze, H. W., *Schott 1953*
Herberigs, Concert champêtre, 1938, *Cebedem*
Herrmann, H., Pastorale Phantasie in op. 51, *Benjamin*
Hess, W., Divertimento op. 51 *Hinrichsen*
Hindemith P., Kleine Kammermusik, op. 24/2 (Fl, Picc), *Schott 1922, AMP*
Hirsch, Quintetto sereno, *Peters*
Höffer, P., Quintett über ein Thema von Beethoven, *Litolff 1947, Peters*
Hohensee, W., *Br & H*
Hoyer, K., Serenade op. 29, *Lengnick, Chester, Simrock 1924*
Huber, K., 3 Sätze (Fl, Picc; Ob, CIngl), *Bä*
Huybrechts, A., 1936, *Cebedem*
Ibert, J., 3 Pièces brèves, *Leduc 1930*

Jacob, G., *By & H*
Járdányi, P., Fantasie, *EMB*
Jersild, J., Serenade, *Hansen*
Jong, M. de, Aphoristisch triptiek, 1953, *Cebedem*
Jungk, K., Chaconne, *Sikorski*
Juon, P., op. 84, *Lienau 1930*
Kadosa, P., op. 49a, *EMB*
Kauffmann, L. J., *UE*
Keith, G. D., *By & H*
Kelemen, M., Études contrapunctiques, *Ars Viva*
King, H., Zimmermann, *Donemus 1954*
Klughardt, A., op. 79, *Zimmermann 1901*
Kodály, Z., Zongora Muzsika Nr. 2, *Elkan*
Kont, P., Quintett in memoriam Fr. Danzi, *Doblinger*
Korda, V., Divertimento, *Doblinger*
Krause, Grumnitz, H., Quintett Nr. 1, *Br & H*
Krenek, E., Pentagramm, *Bä*
Kubizek, A., Kammerquintett, *Doblinger*
Kunert, K., Bläserquintett op. 17, *Hofmeister*
   Divertimento op. 18, *Hofmeister*
   Divertimento op. 14, *Spratt*
Kurtág, G., *EMB*
Ladmirault, P., Choral et Variations, *Lemoine 1952*
Landré, G., *Donemus*
Láng, L., *EMB*
Legley, V., op. 58, 1961, *Cebedem*
Lehmann, H. U., Episoden, *Ars Viva*
Leukauf, R., op. 25, *Doblinger*
Lipatti, Aubade, *Peters*
Lohse, *Peters*
Louel, J., 1958, *Cebedem*
Lucký, Št., *Artia, Prague*
Maasz, G., Finckenschlag, *Sikorski*
McBride, R., Jam Session, *Elkan*
Mederacke, K., Böhmische Suite, *Hofmeister*
Meester, L. de, Divertimento, 1946, *Cebedem*
Meulemans, A., 3 Quintette, 1931, 1932, 1958, *Cebedem*
Meyer-Tormin, W., Kleines Quintett, 1951, *B & B*
Migot, *Leduc*
Milhaud, D., La Cheminée du Roi René, *Andraud 1939*
   Madrigal & Pastorale, *Mercury*
Milner, A., (Fl, Picc), *UE*
Moritz, E., *Zimmermann*

Müller, P., Quintett nr. 1, *Benjamin*
Nevin, E., Gondolieri, *UE*
Nielsen, C., op. 43, *Hansen 1923*
Onslow, G., op. 81, *Br & H, Leuckart*
Parris, H. M., Miniaturen, *Elkan*
Pauer, J., *Artia, Prague*
Petrovics, E., *EMB*
Pierné, G., Pastorale op. 14/1, *Leduc 1939*
Pierné, P., Suite pittoresque, *Leduc 1936*
Pijper, W., *Donemus*
Pilss, K., Serenade, *Doblinger*
Piston, W., *AMP*
Placheta, H., op. 8, Divertimento, *Doblinger*
Porter, Divertimento, *Peters*
Quinet, M., 8 petites pièces, 1946, *Cebedem*
    Quintette op. 54, 1955, *Cebedem*
Rathaus, K., Galante Serenade, *By & H*
Reicha, A., 3 Quintette, *MAB*
    E♭-Dur op. 88,2, *Leuckart*
    B-Dur op. 88,5, *Leuckart*
    D-Dur op. 91,3, *Ric, Peters*
    C-Dur op. 91,1, *Ric, AMP*
    A-Dur op. 91,5, *Ric, AMP*
    E-moll op. 100, *Ric*
    6 Quintette op. 100 (F, C, E♭, E, A, B), *Costallat*
    op. 88, E-moll, *Costallat*
    (18 Quintette op. 88, 91, 99, *Simrock*)
Reiter, A., *Doblinger*
Reizenstein, F., *Hawkes 1937*
Riegger, W., *Ars Viva*
Roetscher, K., op. 41, *B & B*
Rorich, C., op. 58, *Grahl & Nicklas, Zimmermann 1921*
Rota, N., Kleines musikalisches Opfer, *Leduc 1955*
Rousseau, N., op. 54, 1955, *Cebedem*
Schäfer, F., *Artia, Prague*
Schiske, K., op. 24, *Doblinger*
Schmid, H. K., op. 28, *Schott 1921, AMP*
Schmidek, K., op. 31, Sonatine, *Doblinger*
Schoenberg, A., op. 26, *UE 1924*
Schröder, H., Divertimento, *Peters*
Schuller, G., Suite, *McGinnis & Marx*
Schwertsik, K., (Picc, Ob, Cl, Cor, Fag), *UE*
Skorzeny, F., Nachtmusik, *Doblinger*

Souris, Nichtigkeiten, *Leduc*
Sprongl, N., op. 90, *Doblinger*
Stainer, J., Scherzo, *By & H*
Stringfield, L., An Old Bridge, *Leeds*
Sydeman, Quintet nr. 2, *Peters*
Székely, E., *EMB*
Szervánszky, E., *EMB*
Taffanael, C. P., *Leduc*
Takács, J., op. 74, Tafelmusik, *Doblinger*
Thilman, op. 44, *Peters*
Tomasi, H., Quintett, *Lemoine, 1952*
    Variations sur un thème corse, *Leduc 1939*
Trede, Chant des oiseaux, *Peters*
Trojan, V., *Bä*
Uray, E. L., *Doblinger*
Urbanner, E., Etüde, *Doblinger*
Veerhoff, C., *B & B*
Vinter, G., 2 Miniaturen, *By & H*
Voss, F., Capriccioso für Soloflöte und Bläserquartett (Ob, Cl, Cor, Fag),
    Br & H
Walzel, L. M., op. 42 Quintetto impetuoso, *Doblinger*
Weber, A., *Leduc*
Weis, F., Serenade, *Hansen 1941*
Wellesz, E., Suite op. 73, *Sikorski, UE*
Wirth, H., Kleine Clementiade, Scherzo, *Sikorski*
Wuorinen, C., Movement, *UE*
Zelenka, I., Chronologie (Fl, Ob, Bcl, Cor, Fag), *Doblinger*
Zender, H., op. 3, 1950, *B & B*
Zillig, W., Lustspielsuite, *Bä*

R   Other Quintets

1 *Quintets for wind instruments (excluding Q)*

Bach, J. C., 4 Quintette (2 Cl, 2 Cor, Fag), *By & H*
    Bläsersinfonien (2 Cl, 2 Cor, Fag), *Hofmeister*
Berezovsky, N. T., Suite op. 11 (Fl, Ob, Cl, CIngl, Fag), *Ed. Russe*
Dittersdorf, K. D. v., Divertimento (2 Ob, 2 Cl, Fag), *Sikorski 1954*
Domansky, A., (Fl, 2 Cl, Cor, Fag), *Schmidt 1936*
Fitelberg, J., Capriccio (Fl, Ob, Cl, Bcl, Fag), *Balan 1931, Omega 1949*
Flothuis, M., op. 13 (Fl, Ob, Cl, Bcl, Fag), *Donemus*
Gassmann, F., Partita (2 Cl, 2 Cor, Fag), *Doblinger*
Gyrowetz, A., Serenata I und II (2 Cl, 2 Cor, Fag), *Heinrichshofen*
Karg-Elert, S., op. 30 (Ob, 2 Cl, Cor, Fag), *Kahnt 1912*

Knab, A., Serenade (Fl, Ob, 2 Cl, Fag), *Peters*
Meulemans, A., Rapsodie, 1961 (3 Cl, Bcl, A-Sax), *Cebedem*
Mozart, W. A., Adagio K. 411 (2 Cl, 3 Bh), *Br & H*
Premru, R. E., Concertino (Trbne, Fl, Ob, Cl, Fag), *Benjamin*
Rosetti, A., Quintett (Fl, Ob, Cl, CIngl, Fag), *Ric*
Stockhausen, K., Zeitmaße (Fl, Ob, CIngl, Cl, Fag), *UE*

2 *Quintets for wind instruments, strings or accordion*

Bentzon, J., Variazioni interrotti op. 12 (Cl, Fag, V, Va, Vc), *Hansen 1928*
Casella, A., Serenata (Cl, Tr, Fag, V, Vc), *UE*
Haydn, M., Quintetto (V, Va, Cl, Cor, Fag), *EMB*
Kaminski, H., (Cl, V, Va, Vc), *UE 1917*
Kont, P., op. 61/2 Concerto lirico (Fl, Cl, V, Va, Vc), *Doblinger*
Nielsen, C., Serenata in vano (Cl, Cor, Fag, Vc, Cb), *SM*
Niewiadomski, S., Flibbertigibbet (2 Cl, 2 Cor, Cb), *PSPH 1955*
Presser, W., Passacaglia (Cl, Cor, V, Va, Vc), *Benjamin*
Prokofiev, S., op. 39 (Ob, Cl, V, Va, Cb), *Gutheil 1923, By & H*
Slavenski, J., Divertissement (Ob, Cl, V, Va, Cb), op. 6, *Schott*
Šramek, V., Suite (2 Cl, Tr, Fag, Accordion), *Artia, Prague*

S   Sextets

1 *Sextets for piano and wind quintet (flute, oboe, clarinet, horn and bassoon)*

Blumer, T., Sextett op. 45, *Simrock 1922*
Bullerian, H., Sextett op. 38 G-Dur, *Simrock 1925*
David, J. N., Divertimento op. 24, *Br & H 1940*
Dresden, S., Kleine Suite (nach Rameau), *Donemus 1913*
    3. Suite (Fl, Picc; Ob, CIngl), *Donemus 1920*
Görner, Kammerkonzert op. 29, *Peters*
Holbrooke, J., Sextet op. 33a, *Chester 1906*
Jacob, G., Sextet, *Benjamin*
Jongen, J., Rhapsodie op. 70, 1922, *Cebedem*
Juon, P., Divertimento op. 51, *Lienau 1913*
Kahowez, G., Structures, *Doblinger*
Meulemans, A., Aubade, 1934, *Cebedem*
Pijper, W., 1923, *Donemus*
Poulenc, F., Sextet, 1932, *Chester 1945*
Roussel, A., Divertissement op. 6, *Rouart 1905*
Sugár, R., Frammenti Musicali, *EMB*
Tansman, A., La Danse de la Sorcière, *Eschig 1924, Schott, AMP*
Thuille, L., Sextett op. 6, *Br & H 1889, AMP*

2 *Other sextets with piano*

Auric, G., 5 Bagatelles (Cl, Fag, Tr, V, Vc, P), *Andraud*
Berezovsky, N. T., Thema und Variationen op. 7 (Cl, 2 V, Va, Vc, P),
    1926, *Ed. Russe, By & H*
Copland, A., Sextet (Cl, 2 V, Va, Vc, P), *By & H 1952*
Dohnányi, E. v., Sextett op. 37 in C (V, Va, Vc, Cl, Cor, P), *Lengnick*
Falla, M. de, Concerto da camera (Fl, Ob, Cl, V, Vc, Cembalo or P),
    1926, *Eschig 1928*
Martinu, B., Die Küchenrevue (V, Vc, Cl, Fag, Tr, P), *Leduc*
Onslow, G., Sextett op. 30 (Fl, Cl, Cor, Fag, Cb, P), *Br & H, AMP*
Petyrek, F., Sextett (Cl, 2 V, Va, Vc, P), *UE 1921*
Pfitzner, H., Sextett op. 55 (Cl, V, Va, Vc, Cb, P), *Oertel*
Pousseur, H., Madrigal III (Cl, V, Vc, 2 Batt, P), *UE*
Prokofiev, S., Ouvertüre über jiddische Themen op. 34 (Cl, 2 V, Va, Vc,
    P), *UE 1924, By & H*
Schiske, K., Sextett (Cl, 2 V, Va, Vc, P), *UE 1940*

3 *Sextets for two clarinets, two horns and two bassoons*

Beethoven, L. van, Sextett op. 71, *Br & H*
    Marsch in B, *Br & H*
Danzi, F., Sextett E♭-Dur, *Sikorski*
Kelterborn, R., Meditationen, *Heinrichshofen*
Krámár, Fr., Partita, *Hofmeister*
Manicke, D., *Simrock*
Mozart, W. A., Serenade E♭-Dur K. 375, *Musica Rara*
Seiber, M., Serenade, *Hansen*

4 *Other sextets without piano*

Addison, J., Serenade (Fl, Ob, Cl, Fag, Cor, Harp), *OUP*
Baermann, H. J., *see* Wagner
Boisdeffre, C. de, Sextett op. 49 (Fl, Ob, Cl, Cor, Fag, Cb), *Hamelle*
Engel, J., Suite I (Cl, 2 V, Va, Vc, Cb), *UE*
Flothuis, M., Divertimento (Cl, Fag, Cor, V, Va, Cb), *Donemus*
Froschauer, H., (Fl, Ob, 2 Cl, Cor, Fag), *Doblinger*
Heiller, A., Sextett (Ob, Cl, Fag, V, Va, Vc), *UE*
Ibert, J., Jardin de Samos, (Fl, Cl, Tr, V, Vc, Batt), *Heugel 1935*
Janáček, L., Suite Mládi (Fl, Ob, Cl, Bcl, Cor, Fag), *Hudebni Matice 1925,*
    By & H, AMP
Jettel, R., Sextett (Fl, Ob, 2 Cl, Cor, Fag), *Doblinger*
Kabeláč, M., Sextett op. 8 (Fl, CIngl, 2 Cl, Cor, Fag), *Bä*
Karren, L., Humoristische Szenen (Fl, Ob, Cl, Bcl, Cor, Cfg), *Andraud*

Lampersberg, G., Concertino (Cl, Tr, Xyl, Tamb. picc, Tam-Tam), *UE*
Moulaert, R., Concert, 1950 (Fl, Ob, Cl, Fag, Cor, Harp), *Cebedem*
Quinet, M., Ballade, 1962 (Fl, Ob, Cl, Cor, Fag, V), *Cebedem*
Reicha, A., Sextett (2 Cl, 2 V, Va, Vc), *McGinnis & Marx*
Rosetti, A., Parthia in B (Ob, 2 Cl, 2 Cor, Fag), *Denkmäler der Tonkunst in Bayern XXV*
Schaub, H. F., Rondo (Fl, Ob, Cl, Fag, V, Va), *Simrock*
Schmitt, F., Sextett (E♭-Cl, 2 B-Cl, Alt-Cl, Bcl, CbCl in E♭), *Durand*
Spohr, L., Fantasie und Variationen op. 81 (Cl, 2 V, Va, Vc, Cb), *Schmidt*
Stolzenberg, G., Sextett op. 6 (Cl, 2 V, Va, Vc, Cb), *Br & H*
Wagner, R., Adagio (Cl, 2 V, Va, Vc, Cb), *Br & H 1926*

T   Septets

1 *Septets with piano*

Gold, E., Septet (Fl, Ob, Cl, Bcl, Cor, Fag, P), *Benjamin*
Hummel, J., Septett militaire op. 114 (Fl, Cl, Tr, V, Va, Vc, P), *Haslinger 1878, Lienau*
Janáček, L., Concertino, 1926 (P, 2 V, Va, Cl, Cor, Fag; Cl, E♭-Cl), *Hudebni Matice*
Martinu, B., Rondi (Ob, Cl, Fag, Tr, 2 V, P), *Bä*
Mirouze, M., Stück für Septett (Fl, Ob, Cl, Fag, Cor, Tr, P), *Leduc*
Pijper, W., Septett für Fl (Picc), Ob (CIngl), Cl, Fag, Cor, Cb, P, *Donemus*
Schönberg, A., Suite op. 29 (E♭-Cl, Cl, Bcl, V, Va, Vc, P), *UE 1926*
Spohr, L., op. 147 (Fl, Cl, Cor, Fag, V, Vc, P), *Peters 1855, Costallat*
Staempfli, E., Septett (Ob, Cl, Fag, V, Va, Vc, P), *B & B*
Stravinsky, I., Septet, 1953 (Cl, Cor, Fag, V, Va, Vc, P), *By & H*

2 *Septets without piano*

Bach, C. P. E., 6 Sonatas, (2 Fl, 2 Cl, Fag, 2 Cor), *Litolff 1935, Musica Rara*
Beethoven, op. 20 (Cl, Cor, Fag, V, Va, Vc, Cb), *Br & H*
Driessler, Aphorismen (Fl, Ob, CIngl, Cl, Bcl, Cor, Fag), *Bä*
Genzmer, H., Septett (Fl, Cl, Cor, V, Va, Vc, Harp), *Schott*
Hindemith, P., Septett (Fl, Ob, Cl, Bcl, Cor, Fag, Tr), *Schott 1949*
d'Indy, V., Chansons et danses op. 50 (Fl, Ob, 2 Cl, Cor, 2 Fag), *Durand*
Kayn, R., Kammerkonzert (Fl, Ob, Cl, Cor, Fag, Trbne), *Sikorski*
Kont, P., op. 61,3, Septett in gemischter Manier (Fl, Cl, Fag, V, Va, Vc, Cb), *Doblinger*
Kreutzer, C., Grand Septet op. 62 (Cl, Cor, Fag, V, Va, Vc, Cb), *Chester*
Ravel, M., Introduction & Allegro, 1906 (Fl, Cl, 2 V, Va, Vc, Harp), *Durand*

Rosetti, A., Parthia nr. 3 D-Dur (2 Ob, 2 Cl, 2 Cor, Fag), (*Kneusslin,*
  Peters, Br & H) Ric
Stravinsky, I., L'Histoire du Soldat (V, Cl, Fag, Tr, Trbne, Cb, Batt),
  Chester
Villa-Lobos, H., Chôros, nr. 7 (Fl, Ob, Cl, A-Sax, Fag, V, Vc), *Eschig 1928*
Yun, I., Musik für 7 Instrumente (Fl, Ob, Cl, Fag, Cor, V, Vc), *B & B*

U   Octets

1 *Octets for two oboes, two clarinets, two horns and two bassoons*

Beethoven, L. van, op. 103, *Br & H*
  Rondino op. 146, *Br & H, AMP*
Haydn, J., Oktett in F, *Kahnt 1901, International Music Co., N.Y., Marks*
Hoffmeister, F. A., Serenade Eb-Dur, *Ric*
Mozart, W. A., Serenade K. 375 Eb-Dur, *Br & H*
  Serenade K. 388 C-moll, *Br & H*
  Divertimento K. 196c in Eb, *Peters*
  Divertimento K. 196f in B, *Peters*
Mysliveček, J., 3 Oktette, *MAB*
Schubert, F., Menuett und Finale, 1813, *Br & H 1889, AMP*
Stranensky, J. I., Parthie F-Dur, 1800, *Erbe Deutscher Musik, 14*
Uhl, A., Vergnügliche Musik, *UE 1944*

2 *Other octets*

Bach, C. P. E., 6 Sonaten (2 Fl, 2 Cl, 2 Cor, 2 Fag), *Benjamin*
  6 Märsche (2 Ob, 2 Cl, Fag, 2 Cor, Batt), *Marks*
Burkhard, W., Serenade op. 77 (Fl, Cl, Fag, Cor, Harp, V, Va, Cb),
  By & H
Brusselmans, M., Prélude et Fugue, 1923 (Fl, Ob, CIngl, Cl, Bcl, Fag,
  Cor, Tr), *Salabert*
Eder, H., Ottetto breve op. 33 (Fl, Ob, Cl, Fag, 2 V, Va, Vc), *Doblinger*
Fellagara, V., Oktett, 1953 (Fl, Ob, Cl, Fag, Cor, 2 Tr, Trbne), *Edizioni*
  Suvini Zerboni
Ferguson, H., Oktett (Cl, Fag, Cor, 2 V, Va, Vc, Cb), *Hawkes 1934*
Frommel, G., Bläser-Suite op. 18 (Fl, Ob, 2 Cl, Fag, Cfg, 2 Cor),
  Süddeutscher Verlag
Jacob, G., Serenade (2 Fl, 2 Ob, 2 Cl, 2 Fag), *By & H*
Nilsson, B., Zeiten im Umlauf (Picc., Fl, Ob, CIngl, Cl, Bcl, Ten-Sax, Fag)
  UE
Pilss, K., Oktett (Cl, Cor, Fag, 2 V, Va, Vc, Cb), *Doblinger*
Schubert, F., op. 166 (Cl, Cor, Fag, 2 V, Va, Vc, Cb), *Br & H, Costallat,*
  By & H

Spohr, L., op. 32 (Cl, 2 Cor, V, 2 Va, Vc, Cb), *Costallat, Lienau*
Stravinsky, I., (Fl, Cl, 2 Fag, 2 Tr, 2 Trbne), *Ed. Russe 1924, By & H*
Tansman, A., 4 Impressionen (2 Fl, 2 Ob, 2 Cl, 2 Fag), *Leeds*
Thärichen, W., Oktett op. 40 (Cl, Fag, Cor, 2 V, Va, Vc, Cb), *B & B*
Uhl, A., 4 Tanzstücke (Cl, Fag, Cor, 2 V, Va, Vc, Cb), *Doblinger*
Varèse, E., Octandre, 1924 (Fl, Ob, Cl, Cor, Fag, Tr, Trbne, Cb), *Ric 1956*
Wellesz, E., op. 67 (Cl, Cor, Fag, 2 V, Va, Vc, Cb), *UE, Lengnick, Mills*

V   Nonets

1 *Nonets for wind quintet (flute, oboe, clarinet, bassoon, horn) and strings*

Angerer, P., Cogitatio, *Doblinger*
Bořkovec, P., *Artia, Prague*
David, T. C., Konzert, *Doblinger*
Foerster, B., Nonett op. 147 (with V, Va, Vc, Cb), *Hudebni Matice, Bä*
Folprecht, Z., Concertino op. 21, *Bä*
Hába, A., Nonett op. 82, *Bä*
Jaroch, J., Kindersuite, *Bä*
Kubizek, A., op. 26b, Sinfonia da camera (with V, Va, Vc, Cb), *Doblinger*
Novák, J., Baletti a 9, *Bä*
Řidky, J., Nonett op. 32 (with V, Va, Vc, Cb), *Durand 1902, Sadlo 1941*
   2. Nonett op. 39, *Bä*
Spohr, L., op. 31 (with V, Va, Vc, Cb), *Lienau*

2 *Other nonets*

Arrigo, Fluxus op. 7 (Fl, 2 Cl, Fag, Tr, Va, Vc, Cb, Harp), *Peters*
Bräutigam, Kleine Jagdmusik op. 11 (Fl, 2 Ob, 2 Cl, 2 Cor, 2 Fag), *Br & H*
Chemin-Petit, H., Suite für 9 Solo-Instrumente (Ob, Cl, Fag, Batt, 2 V,
   Va, Vc, Cb), *Lienau*
Genzmer, Nonet (Ob, Cl, Fag, Cor, 2 V, Va, Vc, Cb), *Peters*
Goossens, E., Phantasy Nonet op. 40 (Fl, Ob, 2 Cl, 2 Cor, 2 Fag, Tr),
   Curwen 1924
Gounod, C., Petite Symphonie op. 90 (Fl, 2 Ob, 2 Cl, 2 Cor, 2 Fag), *UE*
Ives, C., Scherzo 'Over the Pavements' (Picc, Cl, Fag, Tr, 3 Trbne,
   Batt, P), *Peer 1954*
Kornauth, E., Kammermusik op. 31 (Fl, Ob, Cl, Cor, 2 V, Va, Vc, Cb),
   UE 1925, Doblinger
Krámár, Fr., Nonett op. 79 (2 Ob, 2 Cl, 2 Cor, 2 Fag, Cfg), *Hofmeister*
Schreck, G., Divertimento op. 40 (2 Fl, Ob, 2 Cl, 2 Fag, 2 Cor), *Br & H*
Zillig, W., Serenade II (3 Cl, Cor, Tr, Trbne, 2 V, Vc), *Bä*

W Ten and more Instruments

Birtwistle, H., The World is Discovered (2 Fl, Ob, CIngl, Cl, Bh or Bcl,
2 Fag, 2 Cor), *UE*
Cossart, A., Suite (2 Fl, 2 Ob, 2 Cl, 2 Cor, 2 Fag, Harp), *Heinrichshofen*
Devienne, F., Ouvertüre (2 Fl, 2 Ob, 2 Cl, 3 Fag, 2 Cor, 2 Tr, Trbne,
Timpani), *Hofmeister*
Dvořák, A., Serenade op. 44 (2 Ob, 2 Cl, 3 Cor, 2 Fag, Cfg, Cb, Vc),
Simrock 1879
Hasquenoph, P., Divertissement (Fl, Ob, Cl, Cor, Fag, 2 V, Va, Vc, Cb),
Doblinger
Jadin, L. E., Symphonie (2 Fl, 2 Cl, 2 Fag, Serpent, 2 Cor, 2 Tr, Trbne),
Hofmeister
Mozart, W. A., Serenade B-Dur K. 361 (2 Ob, 2 Cl, 2 Bh, 2 Fag, 4 Cor,
Cfg or Cb), *Br & H*
    Divertimenti Eb-Dur und B-Dur (2 Ob, 2 Cl, 2 CIngl, 2 Cor, 2 Fag),
    Br & H, AMP
Nilsson, B., Zeitpunkte (Fl, Alt-Fl, Ob, CIngl, Cl, Bcl, Ten-Sax, A-Sax,
Fag, Cfg), *UE*
Rawsthorne, A., Concerto for 10 Instruments (Fl, Ob, Cl, Cor, Fag, 2 V,
Va, Vc, Cb), *OUP*
Schönberg, A., Kammersymphonie op. 9 (Fl, Ob, CIngl, D-Cl, Cl, Bcl,
Fag, Cfg, 2 Cor, 2 V, Va, Vc, Cb), 1906, *UE*
Stockhausen, K., Kontrapunkte (Fl, Cl, Bcl, Fag, Tr, Trbne, P, Harp, V,
Vc), *UE*
Strauss, R., Serenade op. 7 (2 Fl, 2 Ob, 2 Cl, 2 Fag, 4 Cor, Cfg), *UE 1884*
    Suite op. 4 (2 Fl, 2 Ob, 2 Cl, 3 Fag, 4 Cor), *Leuckart 1911*
Wranitzky, P., Jägermärsche (2 Ob, 2 Cl, 2 Cor, 2 Tr, 2 Fag, Cfg), *Bä*

X Music for Basset Horn

Birtwistle, H., The World is Discovered (2 Fl, Ob, CIngl, Cl, Bh or Bcl,
2 Fag, 2 Cor), *UE*
Jelinek, H., Divertimento op. 15/8 (Eb-Cl, Cl, Bh, Bcl), *UE*
Klebe, G., 7 Bagatellen op. 35 für Bassetthorn, Posaune, Harfe,
Röhrenglocken, *B & B*
Mendelssohn-Bartholdy, F., 2 Konzertstücke op. 113, 114 (Cl, Bh, P),
Br & H, André, International Music Co. 1957
Mozart, W. A., 12 Duette (2 Bh) K. 487, *Br & H*
    Kanonisches Adagio K. 410 (2 Bh, Fag), *Br & H*
    Adagio K. 411 (2 Cl, 3 Bh), *Br & H*
    Serenade B-Dur K. 361 (2 Ob, 2 Cl, 2 Bh, 4 Cor, 2 Fag, Cfg), *Br & H*

Stark, R., Sonate G-moll (2 Cl, Bh), *Schmidt 1897*
  Serenade op. 55 (2 Cl, Bh, Bcl), *Schmidt 1922*
Tuthill, B., Intermezzo op. 1/2, 1927, (2 Cl, Bh), *C. Fischer 1932*

Y   Music for Bass Clarinet

1 *Bass clarinet and orchestra or piano*

Bontoux, D., Intermezzo, *Andraud*
Bozza, E., Ballade, *Leduc*
Desportes, Y., Andante & Allegro, *Leduc*
Diethe, F., Romanze, *Merseburger*
Galliard, 6 Sonaten, *Peters*
Hoffmann, A., Serenade basque, *Belwin*
Hovey, L., Aria cantando, *Belwin*
  Solo semplice, *Belwin*
  Valse grazioso, *Belwin*
Karel, Aquamarine, *By & H 1955*
Klughardt, A., Romanze für Baßklarinette und Orchester, *Schmidt*
Kühn, J., Adagio aus dem Militär-Konzert (with orchestra), *Schmidt*
Orlamünder, J. G., Romanze, *Schmidt*
Parris, H. M., Nocturne and Burlesque, *Benjamin*
Phillips G., Recitativ und Tanz, *Schott*
Rasse, F., Lied, *Evette & Schaeffer*
Rathaus, K., In Ancient Style, *Belwin*
Schoeck, O., Sonate op. 41, *Br & H 1931*
Thilman, Gestalten, *Peters*
Winsloe, T., Sonatine, *Belwin*

2 *Duets with bass clarinet*

Maschayeki, A., 9 Expressionen (Cl, Bcl), *UE*
Schuller, G., Duo Sonata (Cl, Bcl), *Peters*

3 *Trios with bass clarinet*

Bove, J. H., Andante & Allegro (2 Cl, Bcl), *Leeds*
Mihalovici, M., Sonate op. 35 (Eb-Cl, A-Cl, Bcl), 1933, *Salabert*
Piňos, A., Karikaturen (Fl, Bcl, P), *Artia, Prague*
Thilman, Trio piccolo (Alt-Fl, Bcl, Va), *Peters*

4 *Quartets with bass clarinet*

Eröd, I., Ricercare ed Aria (Fl, Ob, Cor, Bcl), *Doblinger*
Jelinek, H., Divertimento op. 15/8 (Eb-Cl, Cl, Bh, Bcl), *UE*

Lampersberg, G., Quartett (Fl, Bcl, Va, Git), *UE*
Scherber, F., Quartett (Ob, Cl, Bcl, P), *Schmidt 1914*
Stark, R., Serenade op. 55 (2 Cl, Bh, Bcl), *Schmidt 1922*
Uhl, A., Divertimento (3 Cl, Bcl), 1957, *Schott*

5 *Quintets with bass clarinet*

Bowen, Y., Fantasy Quintet (Bcl, 2 V, Va, Vc), *de Wolfe*
Fitelberg, J., Capriccio (Fl, Ob, Cl, Bcl, Fag), *Balan 1931, Omega 1949*
Flothuis, M., Quintett op. 13 (Fl, Ob, Cl, Bcl, Fag), *SD*
Meulemans, A., Rapsodie, 1961 (3 Cl, Bcl, A-Sax), *Cebedem*
Verrall, J., Serenade (3 Cl, Alt-Cl, Bcl), *UE*
Zelenka, I., Chronologie (Fl, Bcl, Cor, Ob, Fag), *Doblinger*

6 *Larger instrumentations with bass clarinet*

Brusselmans, M., Prélude et Fugue, 1923 (Fl, Ob, CIngl, Cl, Bcl, Fag,
    Cor, Tr), *Salabert*
Cerha, F., Exercises für 9 (Bcl, Bar-Sax, Cfg, Cor, Bass-Tr, Trbne,
    Cb-Tuba, Vc, Cb), *UE*
Driessler, Aphorismen (Fl, Ob, CIngl, Cl, Bcl, Cor, Fag), *Bä*
Gold, E., Septet (Fl, Ob, Cl, Bcl, Cor, Fag, P), *Benjamin*
Hindemith, P., Septett, 1948, (Fl, Ob, Cl, Bcl, Cor, Fag, Tr), *Schott 1949*
Janáček, L., Suite Mládi (Fl, Ob, Cl, Bcl, Cor, Fag), *Hudebni Matice 1925,*
    By & H, AMP
Karren, L., Humoristische Szenen (Fl, Ob, Cl, Bcl, Cor, Cfg), *Andraud*
Nilsson B., Zeitpunkte (Fl, Alt-Fl, Ob, CIngl, Cl, Bcl, Ten-Sax, A-Sax,
    Fag, Cfg), *UE*
   Zeiten im Umlauf (Picc, Fl, Ob, CIngl, Cl, Bcl, Ten-Sax, Fag), *UE*
Paccagnini, A., Musica da Camera (Picc, Fl, Bcl, Cor, Vibr, Harp, V, Vc,
    Cb), *UE*
Schmitt, F., Sextett (Eb-Cl, 2 B-Cl, Eb-Alt-Cl, Bcl, Eb-CbCl), *Durand*
Stockhausen, K., Kreuzspiel (Ob, Bcl, P, 3 Batt), *UE*
   Kontrapunkte (Fl, Cl, Bcl, Fag, Tr, Trbne, P, Harp, V, Vc), *UE*
Schönberg, A., Suite op. 29 (Eb-Cl, Cl, Bcl, V, Va, Vc, P), *UE 1926*
   Kammersymphonie, 1906 (Fl, Ob, CIngl, D-Cl, Cl, Bcl, Fag, Cfg, 2 Cor,
    2 V, Va, Vc, Cb), *UE*

Z   Music for Contrabass Clarinet

Landré, G., Konzert für Kontrabaßklarinette und Orchester, *Donemus*
Migot, Prélude pour clarinette contrebasse, *Leduc*
Schmitt, F., Sextett (Eb-Cl, 2 B-Cl, Eb-Alt-Cl, Bcl, Eb-CbCl), *Durand*

INDEX OF SUBJECTS

INDEX OF NAMES